DEDICATION

A Tribute to My Father

Your unwavering belief in the importance of truth has been a guiding light throughout my life.

Your constant encouragement to speak without fear and a firm commitment to honesty have

taught me the value of integrity and the importance of staying true to oneself.

You have inspired and encouraged me to be fearless in speaking my mind.

These values of integrity and authenticity have shaped the person I am today.

With deep gratitude and admiration,

I dedicate this book to you.

AN APPEAL

Let's work to build a Drug-Free Nation.

Dear friends,

The growing drug menace and drug addiction epidemic is impacting countless lives and families across our nation. As the author of "India Drugged-An Eye Opener" I am on a mission to make a difference.

I believe that drug addicts are Sick people and need Treatment-Rehabilitation and not imprisonment.

To support those impacted by drug abuse, I have decided to donate Royalties/profits earned from my book to drug rehabilitation centres.

Every book sold, will contribute towards this Noble cause.

With your support, we can offer a lifeline to those affected by drug abuse and provide much-needed assistance to their families.

Join me in this Noble mission. Together, we can bring hope and healing to those in need and a much-needed positive change and build a brighter future.

Let's work to build a Drug-Free Nation. -Nasha Mukt Bharat

With gratitude,

Monish Bhalla

INDIA DRUGGED

AN EYE OPENER

MONISH BHALLA
-Former NCB Officer

ISBN 979-8-89026-691-0

TAKE A PLEDGE
SAY NO TO DRUGS

Today we are united to take a pledge under the Nasha Mukt Bharat Abhiyaan to make not only our community, family, friends but ourselves drug free because change starts from within, so pledge together to make India Drug Free.

I pledge that I will take all efforts in my capability to make India Drug-Free.

Jai Hind!

Click below and Get a Government certificate

https://nmba.dosje.gov.in/pledge-certificate.php

In Appreciation of Your Support

I would like to take this opportunity to express my gratitude to everyone who played a role in making "India Drugged: An Eye Opener" a reality.

To my dear wife, Alka, I am immensely thankful for her constant support and encouragement throughout the entire writing process. Her belief in me was a constant source of motivation.

My son, Raghuvansh, also deserves a special mention for providing me with invaluable insights and feedback that helped shape the book.

Finally, I want to express my heartfelt appreciation to my Mother for her blessings and unwavering support.

I am also grateful to my dedicated office team, Tulsi and Raj, for their tireless efforts in ensuring that the book was completed to the highest standards.

I cannot thank you all enough for your contributions in making this book a reality. I am truly humbled and grateful.

Warm regards,

Monish Bhalla

Table of Contents

Preface 13
Prologue 15

Section 1
The Drug Menace in India

Punjab: The Udta Punjab 21

Kerala: The Cooking Centre 26

The Northeast States: The Camouflaged Terrain 31

Andhra Pradesh: The Operation Parivartan..............36

West Bengal: The Illegal Migrants 38

Haryana: Punjab in Making......................................40

Gujarat: The Maritime Route...................................42

Karnataka: Bangalore, The IT Brains......................46

Himachal Pradesh: The Chitta-Malana Cream.........49

Delhi: The Central Hub 53

Maharashtra: Mumbai, The Unhealthy Nexus 56

Telangana: The Rave Culture—Youth Disillusioned 60

Uttarakhand: The Pharma Pills 62

Tamil Nadu: The Novel Methods 64

Uttar Pradesh: The Undisputed Leader...................66

Rajasthan: The Border State 68

Madhya Pradesh: The Opium Origin........................70

Odisha: Cannabis Capital of India...........................72

Jharkhand: The Illicit Opium Belt.................................74

Bihar: The Toffee Ganja 76

Jammu-Kashmir: The Narco War 78

Chhattisgarh: The Naxal Ganja...................................81

Goa—The Rússkaya Máfiya...83

Section 2
An Eye Opener

A Calendar of Drug Seizures—The Timeline.........................93

An Eye Opener: Stark Reality....................................... 105

Section 3
Demystifying Drugs: Types and Effects

Drugs of Abuse: Narcotic Drugs Classes and Abuse 115

Cannabis-Based Drugs.. 117

Marijuana 117

Marijuana Consumption 118

Smoke Joint.. 118

Weed Cakes and Chocolates 118

Marijuana Concentrates....................................... 118

Hydroponic Weed 119

Idukki Gold.. 119

Effects of Marijuana on the body and mind 120

Charas – Hashish 120

Hash Oil 121

Malana Cream... 121

Bhang 121

Opioid-Based Drugs.. 122

Opium.. 122

Morphine 124

Heroin 124

Chitta 125

Poppy Husk... 125

Cocaine 126

Khat.. 127

Synthetic Drugs 128

LSD.. 128

Mephedrone.. 129

Methaqualone – Mandrax.. 130

ATS—Amphetamine-Type Stimulants 131

Methamphetamine... 132

Speed 132

Ecstasy 133

Spice 133

Medicinal Prescription Drugs—Misuse and Abuse...... 134

Yaba: The Crazy Drug Craze 135

NPS: New Psychoactive Substances 136

Designer Drugs... 137

Drug-Related Paraphernalia..140

Section 4

In the Shadows of Darknet

Deep Web... 147

The Onion Router (Tor) 148

Darknet Markets.. 148

Darknet Drug Syndicate in India 152

Darkathon 153

Time for a strong cyber-wing 154

Cryptocurrency—An Innovative Drug Currency 155

    Crypto Protocols 155

    Crypto-Cannabis 157

Section 5
Uncovering the World of Drug Smuggling

Modus Operandi—The Art of Concealment 161

Narco-Terrorism—The K2 Factor 166

Drones—A New High-Tech Gadget in the
Hands of Narco-Terrorists 171

Our Neighbors—Double Trouble 175

The Foreign Hand: Nigerians—Reverse Smuggling 179

Illegal Cannabis and Opium Cultivation 183

Hemp—Still in the Nascent Stage 186

Section 6
The Chemistry and Economics of Drugs

Precursors and Pre-Precursors 193

Cooks, Kitchens, and Recipes 197

The Pharma Nexus—A Well-Oiled Network 199

A System Failure—Unbecoming of an Officer 203

Bushy Plant to "Shisha": The Dangerous Industry 207

The Economics of Drugs: Money Matters 213

Money Launderers and Hawala Operators 215

Section 7
The Global Drug Scenario

All Eyes on Afghanistan, Iran, and Pakistan 221

Indian Ocean—An Ocean of Drugs 226

Section 8
Combating Drug Menace

The Road Ahead—Eradicating Drug Abuse 239

"Sick or a Criminal?" 241

Full Body Truck Scanners (FBTS) 249

The Future is Technology and AI: Drug Testing Kits 253

Justice Delayed is Justice Denied 257

Man, Machine, and the Dogs 261

Section 9
Dream of a Drug-Free Nation: Some Positive Steps

Nasha-Mukt Bharat 267

The Endless Debate: Decriminalization,
Depenalization, and Legalization 270

Section 10
Epilogue-Bibliography-Works Cited References

Epilogue 275

Glossary of Drug Lexicon and Abbreviations 277

Bibliography 282

PREFACE

India Drugged is a book that could not have come at a more critical time. The Drug menace and the rising abuse has plagued India. It has serious affects on individuals, families, and communities across the country. The book provides a detailed analysis of the drug situation in India, covering various states and regions, and offers insights into the types of drugs and their effects on the human body and mind. It also delves into the shadowy world of drug smuggling, the chemistry and economics of drugs, and the global drug scenario. It also highlights the role played by drug smugglers and the methods they use to conceal their operations, the use of technology to combat drug trafficking, and the need for a multi-pronged approach to create a drug-free India.

The book is not just informative but is also an eye-opener. It provides a stark reality check for policymakers, law enforcement agencies, and the general public, highlighting the urgent need to address the issue of drug abuse in India. The book serves as a guide for creating a drug-free nation and offers recommendations for eradicating drug abuse, providing treatment to addicts, and strengthening law enforcement agencies.

India Drugged is an must read for anyone who wants to understand the drug situation in India and the urgent need for action. The book is not just for policymakers and law enforcement agencies but also for parents, educators, and anyone who cares about the well-being of society. I highly recommend this book to everyone who wants to create a drug-free India.

PROLOGUE

The cruise drug raid by the Narcotics Control Bureau (NCB) Mumbai and the subsequent arrest of a Bollywood celebrity's son has precipitously brought the focus on the mounting drug menace in our country. Media came in hyper action resulting in unending TV debates, political parties engaging in verbal wars to gain brownie points; personal attacks and character assassination of officers, and unwarranted comparison of state verses central agencies irrespective of both working towards a common goal making India drug free. Amid all the din, it's easy to lose sight of what's important.

A massive consignment (2,988.22 kg) of Heroin, with an estimated street value of ₹21,000 crore, was seized at Gujarat's Adani-owned Mundra Port, by the Directorate of Revenue Intelligence (DRI) in September 2021. The inputs were provided by none other than the National Customs Targeting Centre (NCTC) under the Directorate General of Analytics and Risk Management (DGARM)—India's premium IT intelligence-based directorate. The National Investigation Agency (NIA) took over the investigation and pan-India raids were conducted resulting in the arrest of various persons including many foreign nationals.

Earlier in July 2021, the DRI, in coordination with NCTC and Nhava Sheva Customs seized about 300 kg of Heroin (street/market value ₹ 2000 crore) from two containers at the Nhava Sheva Port in Navi Mumbai.

The seizure of illegal drugs in India has increased exponentially over the past five years, with the darknet and the maritime route becoming the most popular methods of trafficking. The seizure of Heroin in the country has increased from 2,146 kg in 2017 to 7,282 kg in 2021, a 300 per cent increase over the past five years. As with the 172 per cent increase in Opium seizures from 2,551 kg in 2017 to 4,386 kg in 2021, and the 191per cent increase in Marijuana seizures from 3,52,539 kg in 2017 to 6,75,631 kg in 2021, a surge in drug trafficking via the maritime route and the darknet could be observed as well.

The Drug Enforcement Agency (DEA) is doing an excellent job. The officers should be credited, regardless of whether they work for the central government or the state police. The flip side of the coin reveals that there is for sure a sharp increase in drug trafficking activities across India. Indeed, this is an area of concern.

There are two points to consider when looking at the fact that there has been an increase in drug trafficking activity. Indeed, two sides to every coin, and the same holds true for this situation.

First, India is still a transit route and conduit for the ever-increasing supply of narcotics in the oceanic region—Australia and New Zealand—and the traditional drug consumers in the United States, Canada, and the United Kingdom.

Secondly, the other side of the coin requires us to confront the reality that India has become a major consumer of narcotics drugs.

And there is a third perspective to consider: what if both of these are correct?

It's hard to confront the truth. When there are scars all around, it's hard to look in the mirror.

> As a society, we tend to avoid confronting reality because we have an ostrich mentality.

In any case, let's face it. Look at the facts for a moment.

The Union Ministry of Social Justice and Empowerment released a report in 2019 titled "Magnitude of Substance Use in India". It asserts that about 2.1 per cent of the country's population, or 2.26 crore citizens, use opioids. This, too, is a modest estimate. The actual figures could be much higher. Undoubtedly, COVID-19 too has played a crucial role in the past two years.

Let us delve a little deeper to discover the truth.

When we think of states that are particularly vulnerable to drug abuse, we immediately think of one that was once the richest in both material and cultural terms, making it a particularly unfortunate choice as a starting point for this discussion. The most opulent state in India is at risk of losing an entire generation due to drug abuse—Punjab.

The Drug Menace in India

Punjab: The Udta Punjab

One of the most opulent states in India is at risk of losing an entire generation due to drug abuse.

Recent drug-related investigations conducted by governmental authorities such as the National Investigation Agency (NIA), Narcotics Control Bureau (NCB), Directorate of Revenue Intelligence (DRI), Customs, and others all have one thing in common: the state of Punjab.

Recently, DRI and the Gujarat Anti-Terrorist Squad (ATS) seized Heroin—a total of 205.6 kg of Heroin, which has an international market value of 1,439 crore rupees. The consignment came at Gujarat's Kandla Port from Iran's Bander Abbas Port and was declared as "gypsum powder", and it was brought into the country in 17 containers (10,318 bags). The narcotic drugs were hidden in the gypsum powder. It is believed that the shipments came from Afghanistan, Iran, and Pakistan. They entered India through the sea route of Gujarat, with Punjab serving as the final destination. Interestingly, during the investigation, the importer could not be located at the address that was listed in Uttarakhand. To avoid being identified, the importer was always moving to new sites and hiding. However, determined and arduous efforts paid off, and it was determined that the importer was living in a remote village in the province of Punjab. The importer attempted to resist and flee; however, he was apprehended by DRI officers.

Similarly, in another significant seizure, the customs officers in Punjab seized 102 kg of Heroin worth ₹ 700 crore. The narcotic drugs were concealed in a shipment of 'mulethi' (liquorice root) travelling by road from Afghanistan. It entered India over the Attari border in Punjab.

The Border Security Force (BSF), which patrols the India-Pakistan and India-Bangladesh borders, confiscated narcotics worth ₹ 949 crore in the past year. The majority of the drugs were seized near the Punjab border.

There are reports of frequent usage of drones for drug trafficking across the Pakistani border. An old nexus between drug traffickers and Pakistan-based terrorists has given rise to Narco-terrorism.

A study conducted by the community medicine department of the Post Graduate Institute of Medical Education and Research (PGIMER) in Punjab around 1.7 lakh people consume opioids, followed by cannabinoids as well as sedative-inhalant stimulants—a class of pharmacological or prescription drugs being used illicitly. The actual number of drug users may be significantly higher. According to some studies, one in three adolescents is hooked to some form of substance abuse.

In 2020, according to NCRB data, 6,909 cases under the Narcotic Drugs and Psychotropic Substances (NDPS) Act were registered in Punjab, compared to 11,536 in 2019. Eighty per cent or more of drug case suspects in Punjab are at large. What could be the reason for such staggering numbers of absconders? There have been strong allegations of the nexus between drug traffickers, police enforcement, and politicians. Some rogue police officers are part of the distribution network. Since 2014, more than 100 Punjab police officers have been arrested for drug smuggling or abetting the crime, according to a study. It has been observed by India's highest court that the newly elected government must act quickly.

So why is one of the most opulent states in India at risk of losing an entire generation due to drug abuse?

Punjab's addicts have evolved beyond the stereotypes of the state's typically idle or impoverished farmers. There may be cops, housewives, professionals, businessmen, and even rich and bored adolescents among the wide consumer base. Drug traffickers serve a wide range of clientele, from the impoverished and uneducated in rural areas to the well-off and well-educated in the cities.

The drug trade in the state is underpinned by a well-oiled marketing operation.

It's the Punjabi music industry. For years, Punjabi songs have glorified and glamourized drug and alcohol abuse. Songs about drugs and liquor are just as popular as love songs. The film *Udta Punjab* shed light on the prevalence of drug-related imagery in Indian music.

One of the most abused drugs in Punjab is Chitta (adulterated Heroin). The street price of one gram of Chitta may range anywhere between ₹3000 to ₹8000 (depending on its purity) and it's a very expensive habit. The most effective drug dealers are themselves drug addicts.

> A drug addict is the final man in the distribution network and the most driven since he engages in drug distribution to fund his habit.

In 2015, the Ministry of Social Justice and Empowerment (MoSJE) of the Indian government initiated the "Punjab Opioid Dependence Survey" (PODS) to investigate the prevalence of opioid dependency in Punjab. This study, conducted by the National Drug Dependence Treatment Centre (NDDTC) team from AIIMS, New Delhi, in collaboration with the Punjab government's Department of Health and Family Welfare and the Society for Promotion of Youth & Masses (SPYM), focused on 10 districts in the state, namely Bathinda, Ferozepur, Gurdaspur, Hoshiarpur, Jalandhar, Kapurthala, Moga, Patiala, Sangrur, and Tarn Taran.

The survey results revealed a thriving illegal market for opioid drugs in Punjab. The researchers also calculated the average daily expenditure of opioid-dependent individuals on these drugs. By multiplying this expenditure with the estimated number of opioid-dependent people in Punjab, they estimated that dependent individuals are spending around 20 crore rupees (approximately USD 2.7 million) daily on opioid drugs. This staggering figure implies that the annual expenditure on opioid drugs in Punjab amounts to about ₹7,575 crore (approximately USD 1 billion). The information presented is based on an older study, and the current situation in Punjab is even more severe and alarming. The level of addiction within the state has reached critical levels, with drug consumption worth thousands of crore. The figures have likely increased manifold since the time of the original study.

Untimely and unfortunate deaths of young people due to drug overdose are frequently being reported. This is something which cannot be allowed to continue. The narcotics drug trade in Punjab is a multi-crore activity that will continue to increase until serious steps are taken to demolish the network.

KERALA: THE COOKING CENTRE

Kerala is home to drug "cooking centres" and women who get drawn into MDMA trafficking.

According to the number of narcotics cases reported so far in the year 2022, Kerala appears to be following Punjab's pattern. In just four months, Kerala has seen an alarming increase in the number of drug cases compared to prior years. Reports indicate that drug abuse among the normal masses is the main reason for the significant increase in the number of Narcotic Drugs and Psychotropic Substances (NDPS) cases registered by the police. If the current trend continues, the state will surely surpass Punjab in drug cases. About 100 cases were previously registered each month. It has risen to over 2,000 now. The data shows that police registered 24,701 cases under the NDPS Act till November 2022, as against 5,695 cases booked in 2021. Drug misuse has increased dramatically throughout the state. In addition to seizing their property, the Kerala Anti-Narcotics Cell plans to impose a 12-month preventive detention on drug dealers and financiers. According to some reports, key cities in Kerala, particularly Kochi, are emerging as "excellent marketplaces" for certain foreigners to sell "drugs" by hosting underground parties at hotels and resorts. It is believed that the state is becoming a centre for the drug mafia due to its extensive international ties.

In the recent past, Ernakulum Excise Officers seized high-dose synthetic drugs including Cocaine and MDMA from a shipment that arrived at the Foreign Post Office from the Netherlands. Investigations revealed an Italian link to the Kerala-based narcotics trafficker, as well as Himachal connections.

A few months back, customs and excise officials raided 'rave' parties staged at some of the city's finest hotels, arresting several people in the process.

During the raids, drugs such as MDMA, Cocaine, and Ganja, as well as smoking paraphernalia, were recovered. The state is certainly on a new high and Kochi is leading from the front. Several such rave parties, attended by young people from well-to-do families, were also raided by Kerala police and excise. In terms of changing colours, Kochi is possibly South India's most lively metropolis. Kochi, like Pune and Chandigarh, now boasts a cosmopolitan subset of its population.

> Kochi, unlike other cities in Kerala, developed a love for late-night parties many years ago, and narcotics ranging from Ganja to Heroin to LSD have made their way into these high-profile gatherings.

In 2021, Ernakulum had the most cases lodged by the Excise department under the NDPS Act and then Thrissur was followed by Kannur, Idukki, Kasaragod, Kozhikode, and Pathanamthitta. The whole state seems to be gripped by the drug menace.

According to some reports, the illegal sale of narcotic-containing drugs is on the rise. Prescription drugs were being diverted to illegal channels for trade in the Indian states, especially southern states. There are more than 22,000 medical shops in the state, with many selling it illegally without a prescription. Because Phensedyl syrup is less expensive, migrant labourers consume it in big quantities. Drugs containing codeine phosphate, such as Corex and Phensedyl, are frequently marketed without a prescription by medical shops. Caverta and Spasmo Proxyvon pills are popular among college students since they provide rapid bliss and have no odour. The pain reliever drug Fortwin is also widely available in medical stores without a prescription. The state is suffering from a severe shortage of officers to combat the drug epidemic.

Kerala has seen an increase in female drug users, with many of them addicted to MDMA groups. While Kerala has seen an increase in narcotics cases, the increased involvement of women, particularly students aged 22 to 25, has become a matter of concern. During the last two years, 18 young women have been arrested in narcotics cases. Ninety per cent of women imprisoned for drug offences were enrolled in professional courses. The majority of the women arrested were addicts who had become carriers. The majority of the women arrested were members of gangs that trafficked MDMA, also known as Ecstasy or Molly in party circles, Hashish oil, and LSD (Lysergic acid diethylamide) stamps.

> The illegal substances were discovered hidden in the bags or undergarments of ladies riding pillion with men. MDMA and stamps are frequently hidden in intimate regions, making inspection and confiscation difficult.

Kerala is home to drug "cooking centres" and women who get drawn into MDMA trafficking. A cooking centre is a small makeshift laboratory equipped with instruments and certain illegal chemical ingredients are added to imported MDMA, making it stronger and more intoxicating. A cooking centre can be contained in a space a little larger than a bathroom. According to reports, the drug mafia has expanded its reach in Kerala by opening cooking centres in several locations to prepare MDMA narcotics. It is said that African nationals control the wholesale MDMA business in Thiruvananthapuram and Kochi. The agencies are now working together to track down the cooking centres.

The increasing number of young people getting involved in NDPS cases in Ernakulam is a matter of concern, despite several awareness programmes. A total of 256 people under the age of 25 were held in various NDPS cases in Ernakulam in 2022.

Recently, a 13-year-old girl admitted to being used as a drug carrier by a drug mafia in exchange for drugs like MDMA. She had made friends with the members of the drug mafia through Instagram, highlighting the dangers of social media in facilitating criminal activities.

Aside from domestic consumption, the state has emerged as a transit point, mostly via its airports, to destinations such as the Maldives and Sri Lanka. The extensive coastline also provides for drug smuggling under the guise of fishing activity. The state has also had a number of significant drug busts in recent years, in which linkages to international drug trafficking rackets that produce financing for terrorist activities were suspected. Indian Coast Guard and NCB agents worked together earlier to seize 300 kg of drugs, five AK-47 rifles and ammo from a boat off the coast of India. The inquiry was taken over by the NIA because of terrorist ties.

In a significant collaborative effort between the Narcotics Control Bureau (NCB) and the Indian Navy, a substantial quantity of approximately 2,500 kg of highly pure Methamphetamine worth ₹12,000 crore was confiscated in Indian waters near the Kerala Coast. Indian agency successfully intercepted a 'mothership' used for drug trafficking. Codenamed 'Samudragupt', the operation specifically targeted the trafficking of drugs originating from Afghanistan through maritime routes. Kerala coast has become a vital point for drug traffickers, both for internal consumption and further transit to nearby nations.

THE NORTHEAST STATES: THE CAMOUFLAGED TERRAIN

Yaba is believed to be trafficked in large quantities in the NE states and eventually winds up in high-end rave parties across India.

The region shares an international border of 5,182 km (about 99 per cent of its total geographical boundaries) with several neighbouring nations, including Tibet in the north, Myanmar in the east, Bangladesh in the southwest, and Nepal in the west. Arunachal Pradesh, Manipur, Mizoram, and Nagaland all share a border with Myanmar. Sikkim, the latest entrant and the eighth northeast state is bordered by Bhutan, Tibet, and Nepal. The infamous Golden Triangle refers to the area bounded by rural highlands in Myanmar, Laos, and Thailand. India's border with Myanmar is 1643 km long, putting it at risk. As the territory comprises steep mountains in the north, hills and river systems in the south, as well as extensive tropical rainforests, the region's rugged environment offers a formidable obstacle for security agencies to function. Assam has been plagued by insurgency for decades. It is considered that the vast majority of insurgents engage in drug trafficking to fuel their unlawful and anti-national activities. This region is a major problem for the entire nation, as drugs worth billions of rupees are pushed through porous borders and harsh terrains to finally enter other parts of the country, spreading the drug menace in India.

Recently, the governments of Assam and Manipur have taken significant measures to combat the drug problem. In a recent raid, Guwahati police seized 205 soap cases containing around 2.5 kg of Heroin worth approximately ₹17 crore. Previously, they seized 1.4 kg of Heroin worth approximately ₹9 crore being shipped by another gang. A narcotics dealer was apprehended with 8,500 Yaba (Meth) tablets.

However, the situation is considerably more extensive than one might believe.

> Myanmar is now believed to be the largest producer of illicit drugs Yaba. Yaba is a tablet-based mix of caffeine and Crystal Meth (Methamphetamine) that is particularly popular with subcontinent party drug users.

This Yaba is believed to be trafficked in large quantities in the NE states and eventually winds up in high-end rave parties across India.

NE is also a major route for the smuggling of codeine-based cough syrup (CBCS) to Bangladesh. In past a major Indian pharmaceutical company was booked by the agencies as their management was said to be involved in such illegal activities. The cough syrup shipments are believed to have originated in the northern Indian states of Himachal Pradesh and Uttarakhand. Even Yaba from illegal laboratories in Myanmar is being trafficked into Bangladesh via NE. It's believed that Bangladeshi druggies consume two million tablets per day. This demonstrated the magnitude of drug trafficking in the area.

The border between Tripura and Mizoram is often exploited for drug trafficking. According to recent reports, the Tripura frontier of the BSF captured 4.67 lakh Yaba tablets, 5 MT of Ganja, and 65,885 bottles of Phensedyl medications. They also destroyed 46 lakh Ganja saplings. It's learned that even the local police arrested, close to 125 persons, were involved in drug abuse and trafficking.

Manipur has had a longstanding drug problem due to its location along an ancient trade route that connects it to Southeast Asia and the infamous Golden Triangle.

This has led to high levels of drug addiction problems in the state, which has been compounded by youth frustration, leading some to choose drugs.

Recently, the problem has taken on a new dimension as illegal poppy cultivation has become prevalent in the hills of Manipur.

This has led to deforestation and environmental damage, as well as conflicts between forest administrators and villagers who have encroached into protected forests for poppy cultivation. As a result, Manipur is at risk of becoming a source of drugs rather than just a transit route for the international drug trafficking network.

For decades, Manipur has been plagued by drug usage and drug trafficking. The state government has only lately begun to operate. According to reports, enormous tracts of forest land were utilized for illicit poppy farms, resulting in the production of Opium worth billions of rupees. This was converted into Heroin in Myanmar. The funds were utilized to fuel the insurgency and anti-national activities. Recently the state CM has claimed 380 acres of poppy cultivation have been destroyed in Manipur. Drugs worth over ₹182 crore have been seized by security agencies in Manipur.

For more than four decades, drug abuse as well as drug trafficking has been a problem in northeastern states. Currently, the situation appears to be better than it was previously. Illicit poppy cultivation and Heroin production, aided by the previous rule of insurgents, were rampant. The procurement of Acetic Anhydride, one of the most crucial chemicals required to convert Opium into Heroin, was facilitated by fictitious pharmaceutical firms. Hundreds of MT of Opium/Heroin were being illicitly produced and smuggled in the camouflaged terrain of NE. A few decades ago, it was believed that the region included tens of thousands of drug users; however, it appears that this number has substantially decreased at present. But, an in-depth survey in the specified region can provide actual facts. However, the newfound craze of Yaba seems to be ever-growing. In January 2023, the Assam police made the largest-ever seizure of Yaba tablets in the state, confiscating over 7.59 lakh tablets worth ₹40 crore in the international market. The recovery was made in the Karim Ganj district of the Barak Valley region. Prior to this, there were several other seizures of Yaba tablets in the state. In November, the authorities recovered 60,000, 20,000, 16,000, and 21 lakh Yaba tablets in separate incidents. In December, another two lakh Yaba tablets were confiscated. The latest seizure of 17,000 suspected Yaba tablets, worth ₹1.70 crore was made near the Harinagar border outpost of the BSF, which is located approximately 16.2 km from India's borders with Bangladesh.

Andhra Pradesh: The Operation Parivartan

Illicit cultivation of the Ganja crop on 7,552 acres worth 9,251 crore was destroyed.

A novel method of drug trafficking was detected in early 2022. Under the guise of stevia leaves, two crore worth of Cannabis (ganja) was illegally marketed online on several e-commerce platforms using forged GSTN numbers from Andhra Pradesh to the states of Rajasthan and Maharashtra. Nine people have been arrested in connection with the racket; the NCB is investigating.

Andhra Pradesh is one of the major producers of Cannabis.

According to official estimates, the narcotic Marijuana is cultivated on more than 10,000 acres spread across 250 tribal villages in these areas bordering Odisha.

In the year 2021, Andhra Pradesh recorded the seizure of more than 1,90,000 kg of Cannabis-based drugs, including ganja.

Operation Parivartan was launched in response to a series of instances of Ganja smuggling from Visakhapatnam forest regions into neighbouring Telangana and Chhattisgarh.

Approximately two lakh kilos of processed Cannabis were intercepted while being sent out after harvest. A total of 1,500 persons have been arrested as part of Operation Parivartan. There were 562 people from different states among them. The police conducted multiple operations in and around the Andhra Pradesh-Odisha border in the Visakhapatnam district, which is notorious for Ganja growing. Police confiscated and destroyed drugs worth more than ₹1500 crore. It is reported that as part of Operation Parivartan, 406 special teams destroyed a Ganja crop worth 9,251 crore on 7,552 acres spread across 11 agency mandals.

Andhra-Odisha belt has been a huge source of **Ganja-Marijuana**. Chennai police have seized 200 kg of Ganja that was smuggled into the state from Andhra Pradesh, in a recent crackdown in February 2023. On April 8th, 2023, in the Anakapalli district of Andhra Pradesh, a team from the NCB seized Ganja weighing over 1,000 kg in the Regupalem area, which falls under the jurisdiction of the Yelamanchali Police Station.

West Bengal: The Illegal Migrants

West Bengal is a potential point of entry and exit for narcotic drugs.

The Siliguri Corridor, also referred to as the Chicken's Neck, is a land passage that runs through the city of Siliguri in West Bengal, India. It is 20-22 km wide at its narrowest point and serves as a crucial geo-political and geo-economic corridor linking the eight northeastern states of India to the rest of the country. West Bengal shares its borders with the countries of Bangladesh, Nepal, and Bhutan, as well as the Indian states of Odisha, Jharkhand, Bihar, Sikkim, and Assam This makes West Bengal a potential point of entry and exit for narcotic drugs.

The NCB recently recovered 20 kg of the strongest Marijuana in the world with a high THC (tetrahydrocannabinol) content, smuggled into India from the United States.

Several courier companies in Kolkata were being used to carry imported Marijuana into the city over the darknet. Recently, the agencies seized drugs worth 100 crore from Murshidabad, a popular transit point for Yaba drug trafficking.

Previously, three college students and a woman were caught in Kolkata with 300 g of Heroin. The Kolkata police confiscated approximately 5.177 kg of Heroin with a market value of ₹25 crore. In December 2022, the Kolkata police uncovered a drug trafficking operation within the city. The authorities made this discovery after confiscating an ambulance that was transporting over 50 kg of drugs.

The Siliguri Metropolitan Police has been carrying out anti-narcotics drives in different areas in Siliguri from October 2022 to February 2023. As a result, they seized a large quantum of drugs, including Cannabis, Brown Sugar, cough syrup, tablets, and injections, worth ₹25 crore in total. The drives were conducted in several police stations, including Pradhan Nagar, Matigara, Bagdogra, Bhaktinagar, Siliguri, and New Jalpaiguri.

Back in October of 2022, the Kolkata police's Special Task Force (STF) confiscated 3,600.7 kg of Poppy Straw from a warehouse in Kolkata. This substance, which is a type of Opium-based narcotic, is valued at approximately ₹30 crore in the market. Additionally, in October, the Kolkata police also discovered 531 kg of Poppy Straw in central Kolkata.

Haryana: Punjab in Making

More than seven lakh addicts have been registered at de-addiction centres in Haryana in seven years.

A statement by the Haryana State Police highlighted that they seized 19,036 kg of narcotics, including Heroin, Charas, Sulpha, Smack, Opium, Poppy Husk, and Marijuana, during the first 11 months of 2021 as a result of an intense crackdown on drug possession and distribution.

Six hundred and eleven persons have been arrested under the Narcotic Drugs and Psychotropic Substances (NDPS) Act during the past nine months in Sirsa district alone followed by Gurugram with 204, Fatehabad with 186, Karnal with 175, Rohtak with 130, Hisar with 113, and Kurukshetra with 113. As an effective deterrence against the menace, the police are making a concerted effort to seize the movable and immovable property of those detained in cases registered under the NDPS Act. This is in addition to their broad crackdowns on drug dealers. The neighbouring state of Punjab has had a considerable impact on the number of people addicted to opioids and synthetic drugs in this state.

Tramadol is an opioid analgesic belonging to the same pharmacological family as oxycodone and hydrocodone. In April 2018, the government designated it a psychotropic substance due to its misuse for addiction purposes. Preventive and Intelligence Cell, Central Bureau of Narcotics,

New Delhi, recently searched a front office in Sirsa that was being utilized as a conduit for the diversion of manufactured tramadol pills disguised as Ayurvedic medicines. Earlier, the Haryana Anti-Narcotics Cell confiscated from a Karnal-based narcotics trafficker 39,600 tramadol capsules and 33,600 alprazolam tablets. To determine the severity of an epidemic in any area, one can look at the figures reflected in doctor's clinics and hospitals. Similarly, the number of drug addicts visiting de-addiction centres is an indicator of the rise in substance abuse and drug menace in a state. In the past seven years, over 7.12 lakh addicts registered at de-addiction centres in Haryana, with over one lakh enrollments reported annually from 2018.

However, it is an open secret that only a few drug addicts seek de-addiction programmes, which highlights the extent of the drug menace affecting the youth of Haryana. Haryana is truly Punjab in making.

Gujarat: The Maritime Route

Three thousand kilos of pure Heroin valued at more than ₹21,000 crore were seized at Gujarat's Mundra Port.

The extensive coastline of Gujarat presents significant maritime issues for the state government, which has acknowledged an increase in Heroin seizures of 10 folds in the last two years. It has now been recommended that the Indian Coast Guard consider employing drones for surveillance and interception of the country's coastlines. The recommendation was made during the NCB's third meeting of the top-level committee of the Narco Coordination Centre (NCORD) in New Delhi. The NCORD was established in 2016 by the Union Ministry of Home Affairs to improve drug law enforcement and effective cooperation among anti-drug trafficking organizations.

It is estimated that more than 70 per cent of total drug trafficking is being conducted through maritime routes. This indicates the gravity of India's current problem and the challenges it is facing.

In September 2021, the DRI recovered 3,000 kg of pure Heroin valued at more than ₹21,000 crore from Gujarat's Mundra Port. The catch has been described as its "largest haul" to date. The international street market price of the contraband is reported to be around ₹7 crore per kg. The Afghan Heroin was transported into the country via the Bandar Abbas Port in Iran and was classified as "semi-processed talc stones".

In February 2023, the NIA filed its second supplementary charge sheet against seven companies and 15 individuals concerning the seizure of 2,988.2 kg of Heroin, which was concealed as talc, at Mundra Port in September 2021. During the investigation, it was discovered that a foreign-based narcotic syndicate was involved in importing Heroin-laden consignments into Mundra and Kolkata ports, which were then diverted to New Delhi.

The investigation uncovered an organized criminal conspiracy to smuggle illegal Heroin consignments through international trade routes to India from Afghanistan, which was hatched by the accused. The authorities also discovered a well-oiled network of operatives involved in the import, facilitation, and transport of drug-laden consignments.

> The investigation revealed that the consignments were being imported through multiple fake/shell import proprietorship firms floated in India by multiple accused individuals.

The investigation further established that an India-based network of Afghan nationals was responsible for hiring these warehouses and processing/extracting and distributing the Heroin once it reached New Delhi. The funds generated through the sale proceeds of Heroin were provided to operatives of Lashkar-e-Taiba (LeT) for the furtherance of terrorist activities in India through hawala operators.

The Gujarat Anti-Terrorism Squad (ATS) confiscated 120 kg of Heroin from Zinzuda town in the state's Morbi district in November 2021. The shipment was initially concealed in a seaside location near the town of Salaya in the Devbhumi Dwarka district, and the Heroin was intended for delivery to an African nation.

A Pakistani fishing boat carrying 77 kg of Heroin worth around ₹400 crore was captured in Indian waters off the Gujarat coast. Earlier in a joint operation, the NCB and the navy had seized around 750 kg of drugs from a ship off the Gujarat coast.

In a joint operation with the Indian Navy, the NCB seized 529 kg of very high-grade Hashish, 234 kg of finest quality Crystal Methamphetamine, and some number of Heroin drugs worth ₹2,000 crore from the high seas near Porbandar off the Gujarat coast.

In April 2022, Gujarat's ATS, in collaboration with the DRI, confiscated around 260 kg of Heroin worth ₹1,500 crore at the Kandla Port in Gujarat's Kutch area. According to reports, the cargo originated from Afghanistan via Iran.

The Gujarat ATS and the DRI confiscated nearly 90 kg of Heroin valued at ₹450 crore from a shipping container arriving from Iran at the Pipavav Port in the Amreli district.

To avoid detection, the drug syndicate developed a novel procedure in which threads were soaked in a Heroin solution, dried, moulded into bales, and packed in bags for export.

A forensic examination of four suspicious bags containing roughly 395 kg of threads indicated that the threads contained opiate compounds or Heroin. In recent years, the Gujarat coast has become a favoured route for the smuggling of high-quality Heroin intended for domestic use and other international markets.

In March 2023, the ICG apprehended an Iranian boat with five crew in Indian waters, near Okha, carrying 61 kg Heroin worth ₹425 crore.

Ahmedabad police discovered a highly organized drug trafficking ring that accepted crypto-currency payments and delivered drugs by air freight couriers. The duo who were running this drug racket were highly qualified and from well-to-do families. Smuggled drugs worth over ₹100 crore were discovered during the preliminary investigation. They sold drugs including hybrid Ganja, American Charas, Malana Charas, and Psychotropic Magic Mushrooms and catered to college students in Ahmedabad and Gandhinagar from a variety of institutions.

Ahmedabad Customs seized 639 pills of the party drug Ecstasy worth more than ₹14 lakh from parcels arriving at the Foreign Post Office. Ecstasy or Molly are used by youngsters in high-end rave parties.

Small quantities of seizures of Kashmiri Charas are very frequent in major cities of Gujarat and most of the Charas addicts are of labour class.

Karnataka: Bangalore, The IT Brains

Food delivery partners deliver drugs to consumers' doorsteps.

In 2021, Bengaluru police arrested 5,644 drug peddlers in 4,275 cases and seized drugs worth around 59 crore. This has been the most narcotics-related arrests and recoveries in the city police department's history. According to data, 4,275 of the 4,475 cases documented in 2021 were due to Marijuana seizures, followed by 103 cases of MDMA, 39 cases of synthetic narcotics, and other narcotic substances such as Ecstasy, Hashish, and LSD. So, on average, more than 100 drug peddlers-addicts are apprehended in Bengaluru city each week. This demonstrates the severity of the city's drug problem.

A Bengaluru MBBS student, a fashion designer, and a finance consultant were amongst the 22 people who were arrested for drug trafficking on the dark web, as a result of nationwide raids by NCB.

Single-use crypto wallets, professional packaging, concealment in articles and use of Indian post and courier services, advertisement on Telegram group, Instagram, fake addresses, vendors verified by owner/co-owner, and no cheating or fraud principle were among the unique aspects of the racket's modus operandi. In a nutshell, the drug trafficking operations were carried out with extreme professionalism.

The NCB in Bengaluru discovered a big narcotics network that allegedly used partners with a meal delivery app to transport high-grade Marijuana in little packets to consumers' doorsteps using Swiggy food delivery partners to deliver drugs in minuscule quantities, as little as 10-50 grams each packet to their consumers. In total, 140 kg of high-grade Marijuana was seized. This drug cartel took advantage of the lockdown by allowing delivery employees to operate. The syndicate thrived, especially with doorstep delivery during the lockdown.

Meanwhile, Karnataka has a unique problem with foreigners overstaying their visas in the state, particularly Nigerians who arrived at the state on student visas and subsequently elect to overstay. It has been discovered that the majority of these immigrants are active in drug dealing among the student population. In 2021, 173 foreign nationals were detained, with 137 complaints brought against them; 105 of the perpetrators were Nigerians.

The NCB confiscated three-kilo narcotics worth crore in Bengaluru during a big operation. The cargo was hidden in three lehengas, and the material confiscated is suspected to be a banned narcotic, pseudoephedrine, which was extracted after opening each fold of the three lehengas' fall line.

In February 2023, a drug case that has come to light in coastal Karnataka revealed some shocking details. Sources report that the substances made their way into the students' rooms through online food deliveries.

> As many as 24 people were arrested in the case, of which 22 were from the medical fraternity, including doctors from Uttar Pradesh, Karnataka, Kerala, Telangana, and New Delhi.

The students, who were mainly in their 20s and 30s, were consuming drugs like MDMA, LSD, and Ganja, and some were also involved in drug peddling. The police department has suspended 42 students for a month in the neighbouring Udupi district, which is known as an education hub. Activists in Belagavi have reported that various colleges and coaching centres openly sell Ganja and other narcotic substances to young students. Many students have become addicted to these drugs, which has had a detrimental impact on their lives and careers.

HIMACHAL PRADESH: THE CHITTA-MALANA CREAM

High-quality Charas-Malana cream is the most sought-after for foreign tourists.

The Government of India's Ministry of Social Justice and Empowerment (MoSJE) commissioned a National Survey on the Extent and Pattern of Substance Use in India. The report indicates that a significant number of people in India use psychoactive substances, and that substance usage exists in all population segments. The National Drug Dependence Treatment Centre (NDDTC), All India Institute of Medical Sciences (AIIMS), New Delhi, was tasked with leading the technical and scientific aspects of the National Survey, which was carried out in all 36 states and union territories of the country in collaboration with ten other medical institutes and a network of 15 non-governmental organizations (NGOs).

The average number of people using Charas and Ganja in the country, according to the survey, is 1.2 per cent. However, 3.2 per cent of the people in Himachal Pradesh are hooked on these drugs, which is almost three times the national average.

Similarly, 1.7 per cent of individuals in Himachal Pradesh take opioids, which is more than double the national average of 0.7 per cent.

Himachal Pradesh's drug problem includes illegal Cannabis and Opium growing. Kullu is well-known for its illegal Cannabis farming.

> The valley's high-quality Charas-Malana Cream is sought after in both foreign and domestic tourism destinations.

Chitta (diacetylmorphine), a semisynthetic opioid, is a kind of Heroin that has been adulterated and is highly addictive. Occasionally, consumers develop an addiction. It is extremely deadly, and an overdose could potentially be fatal.

> Himachal is following Punjab's footsteps by becoming dependent on this lethal drug.

Chitta has made inroads even in the rural areas of tourist-heavy regions, particularly in Shimla, Kangra, Una, Sirmaur, and Solan. The situation is worse in the regions bordering Punjab.

Kasol, a small town in Parvati Valley, seems to be a popular destination for drug tourists, offering a wide variety of opiates, Cannabis, and the contaminated form of Heroin known as Chitta. The town also serves as a gateway to Malana, known internationally for high-grade Malana Cream Heroin. Unfortunately, drug trafficking is becoming a menace in these areas and it is an abuser's destination, for attending rave parties or getting high.

The National Crime Record Bureau (NCRB) report on "Crimes in India in 2020" says that over 1,500 drug abuse and trafficking cases were registered in Himachal in 2020.

It appears that the vast majority of the instances of drug trafficking included seizures of Cocaine, Heroin, Brown Sugar, Opium seeds, Charas, Marijuana, MDMA, and LSD papers/stamps.

As a result, it is no longer just drugs grown locally. Drug traffickers are smuggling substances of abuse to this tourist destination state. In the past seven years, drug-related cases have surged by more than threefold. As instances were booked across the state in Chamba, Bilaspur, Shimla, Kullu, Kangra, Mandi, Una, and Solan, the data suggest that drugs have penetrated deep into the hilly state.

In Himachal, three types of narcotic drug networks are functioning. One is run by Punjab-based traffickers, another by Africans, and the third by Uttar Pradesh-based smugglers.

In this hill state, 72 foreign nationals were arrested between 2017 and 2021 for their involvement in drug trafficking. According to police records, 36 were Nigerian nationals, followed by 15 from other African nations, 14 Europeans, four Americans, two from the Middle East, and one from Asia. In the past five years, the state police have arrested 8,122 Indian nationals and 80 foreigners for violating the NDPS Act of 1985.

Drug trafficking in Himachal Pradesh has become a major concern, with daily seizures reported in districts such as Kangra, Shimla, Kullu, and Una. In a crackdown on drug trafficking in Shimla, 190 people have been arrested, including 45 from out of state, with 97 cases related to the narcotic Chitta (Heroin) in less than a month. A recent police workshop revealed that drug peddlers are targeting educational institutions, coaching centres, and hostels to recruit youths for drug abuse and peddling.

> Private rehabilitation centres have also come under police scrutiny as drugs are easily accessible to addicts.

Failure to take immediate action may result in an uncontrollable situation leading to a catastrophic crisis for future generations.

Delhi: The Central Hub

Rupees 1200 crore drugs seized from an Afghan drug cartel.

The NCB busted an India-Afghanistan drug syndicate and seized about 50 kg of "high-quality" Heroin from the Shaheen Bagh area of Jamia Nagar in one of Delhi's largest narcotics seizures. The NCB also seized 47 kg of other suspected drugs and ₹30 lakh in cash and arrested many foreigners during the investigation.

Customs officers at Indira Gandhi International (IGI) Airport seized 5.85 kg of Cocaine, the largest seizure at any Indian airport in the last six months. IGI Airport alone has had approximately 16 cases booked under the NDPS Act, the most for any airport. During the years 2021–2021, nearly 33.70 kg of Heroin and 12.60 kg of Cocaine were seized from international passengers, the majority of whom were of African descent, with a street value of ₹ 887.35 crore.

Revenue Intelligence officers seized 62 kg of Heroin worth ₹434 crore at the IGI Airport air cargo complex, making it one of the largest such seizures to date.

The DRI seized 55 kg of Heroin from an imported cargo consignment that was declared to contain 'trolley bags' in an operation code-named 'Black & White'. The drugs were concealed inside 126 trolley bags with hollow metal tubes, making detection extremely difficult.

Previously, Delhi police recovered 150 kg of Heroin from a processing lab in Delhi, which was destined for high-demand markets such as Punjab, as well as transnational movement through the southern states to Sri Lanka and eventually other territories.

Two distinct methods were observed in such airport seizures. Some passengers pack drugs inside latex capsules, which they swallow to get past customs officers easily at the airport. Later, they eject these capsules after consuming laxatives, running a great risk to their own lives. This modus operandi is not only difficult to detect, but also difficult to retrieve, as suspected passengers need to be admitted to government hospitals where the extraction is conducted under medical supervision, often taking four to five days or longer. In the second method, drugs are concealed in specially made cavities in hand baggage or checked-in baggage being carried by passengers. Such cases are detected by the combined use of the Customs Canine Squad and high-resolution X-ray. Both these methods have been detected at IGI Airport.

In September 2022, two Afghan nationals were arrested by the Special Cell from Delhi's Southeast district in an alleged drug cartel bust. The police seized 312.5 kg of Methamphetamines and 10 kg of Heroin was the largest seizure ever made, with an estimated international value of over ₹1,200 crore. The presence of ephedra plants in Afghanistan has provided a low-cost method to extract ephedrine and make Methamphetamines from it, which has replaced Heroin as the drug of choice. The expanding market and the remunerative lucrativeness have ensured that there is no reduction in the relentless flow of drugs attempted to be smuggled into India through the airports. Drugs having an international market worth more than ₹40 crore were seized in March 2023, when Delhi's Special Cell found high-quality pure Heroin that was hidden in a Scorpio vehicle, including door panels, the stepney, and 224 soap boxes.

The NIA is investigating a potential link between narcotics and terrorism in Delhi, which is a cause for concern given the presence of VIPs and prominent individuals.

> A Page 3 celebrity and Delhi clubbing tycoon was apprehended by the NIA for his alleged involvement in a drug smuggling operation. He is suspected to have smuggled hundreds of kilos of Heroin into India from Afghanistan after a Pakistan-backed syndicate stockpiled the drug during the COVID-19 pandemic.

His activities were discovered following the 2021 Mundra Port drug bust, and the NIA has a detailed charge sheet of the methods he used to smuggle the contraband through Indian ports. He is alleged to have been handsomely compensated for his services, which were meant to fund terror activities of Lashkar-e-Taiba (LeT) and Hizbul Mujahideen.

As per the National Survey on the Extent and Pattern of Substance Use in India, there are 8.12 per cent Cannabis addicts, 7.79 per cent Opioid addicts, and a high proportion of Amphetamine, hallucinogen, inhalant, and injectable drug addicts in Delhi. These figures are significantly higher than the national average. These are government figures; one can make an educated guess as to what the actual figures will be. Unfortunately, Delhi appears to be headed for a drug abuse catastrophe.

Maharashtra: Mumbai, The Unhealthy Nexus

Mumbai is no stranger to drug trafficking and the drug mafia.

In the much-hyped Aryan Khan cruise drug case, his childhood friend Arbaaz Merchant and many other guests were caught with Cocaine, Charas, Hydroponic Weed, and MDMA. The drug mafia and Bollywood nexus are back in the spotlight. In 2020, there were 3,509 NDPS cases booked in Mumbai.

As per "Crime in India 2020", Mumbai accounts for 30 per cent of the 12,010 NDPS Act cases reported in 19 major cities.

In just the first four months of 2022, Mumbai police seized 550 kg of drugs and arrested 2897 people. It shows that, on average, more than 30 people are arrested every day for drug-related crimes.

Mumbai is no stranger to drug trafficking and the drug mafia. Law enforcement agencies have seized a wide range of narcotics, including Charas, Marijuana, Heroin, and designer drugs. A novel modus operandi is used to smuggle drugs.

Earlier in July 2021, the DRI, in coordination with the National Customs Targeting Centre and Nhava Sheva Customs, seized about 300 kg of Heroin worth ₹2000 crore from two containers at the Nhava Sheva Port in Navi Mumbai.

Two people were recently arrested in Dombilvili; Cannabis was grown there using hydroponic techniques. Water pumps, air circulation systems, and photosynthesis lighting systems were all part of the cultivation setup. Two Germans were caught growing Cannabis in a bungalow in Satara Hills in February 2021.

At Mumbai Airport, a customs official arrested a Zimbabwean woman for smuggling Heroin and the illegal drug Methamphetamine, also known as Meth, worth ₹60 crore. They also discovered 27 kg of high-quality hydroponics Marijuana hidden in a variety of household items, including an outdoor waterfall, a fake wood leather chair, and a propane gas fire pit table. A package was intercepted, and 910 grams of Marijuana from California were found hidden in an air purifier. In another case, 35 kg of Heroin worth more than ₹240 crore was seized from two Zimbabweans who were arrested at Chhatrapati Shivaji Maharaj International Airport (CSMIA). The NCB seized 1,127 kg of Marijuana (Ganja) in Manjram, Nanded. In Bhiwandi, Thane, they recently seized 864 kg (8640 bottles) of CBCS. Recently, Weed Cakes and Weed Pot Brownies were seized from a bakery in Malad, Mumbai, showing a new trend in Mumbai youngsters and novel ways to consume Cannabis.

Mumbai is also the capital of both Bollywood and Cricket. Cinema and Cricket have been a source of obsession for Indians, with the youth looking up to them as their heroes. The level of craze is unparalleled, with some individuals even regarding these stars as Gods. The younger generation is greatly influenced by these stars, to the extent that they emulate them in various aspects of their lives, including fashion and lifestyle. If one of their idols crosses the line and falls into drug abuse, some young people may view it as a cool thing to imitate. Both Bollywood and Tollywood have numerous examples where celebrities have been found on the wrong side of the law. The cricket world is no exception, as many cricket stars from around the world have faced accusations of drug abuse. A recent example is Wasim Akram, who admitted in his latest book to having struggled with drug addiction. Sanjay Dutt, a Bollywood star, is also known for his drug problems.

> The cruise drug case brought to light the involvement of many influential members of society and Page 3 celebrities in drug-related activities.

The NCB has filed charges against 14 individuals, including Aryan Khan's friend Arbaaz Merchant.

Over the past few years, after Sushant Sigh Rajput's mysterious death, many Bollywood celebrities have been questioned by the NCB, highlighting the prevalence of drug culture and rave parties within closed circles that are no longer a secret.

The film industry is a highly influential medium that can have a significant impact on society. Film stars must know that the larger their fan following, the greater the responsibility on their shoulders to ensure that their behaviour and lifestyle do not have any negative influence on their fans or society as a whole.

Mumbai has been knee-deep in narcotic drugs for decades. The drug mafia cannot thrive in the absence of a likely *Babu-Neta-Cop* nexus and Mumbaikars know-it-all.

Telangana: The Rave Culture—Youth Disillusioned

The youth think that drugs are cool and a creativity booster.

Two African nationals were apprehended for smuggling ₹80 crore worth of Cocaine at Rajiv Gandhi International Airport, Hyderabad. They had concealed four kilos of Cocaine in packet form in the false bottom of their trolley bags. Since the formation of the Hyderabad Narcotics Enforcement Wing (H-NEW), 120 individuals, including 30 drug dealers, have been arrested. At least 2,500 grams of Hashish oil, 43 blots of LSD, and nearly 25 kg of Marijuana have been seized to date.

The NCB busted a Hyderabad-based internet pharmacy group that was diverting psychotropic medications for recreational use to the United States. The NCB also seized ₹3.71 crore in cash and several electronic devices.

In Hyderabad, rave parties are becoming more common. The Radisson Blu Hotel's Pudding & Mink Hotel was the target of a police raid in Hyderabad. The police have seized five sachets of white powder they believe to be Cocaine.

> A total of 148 people, including the children of prominent politicians and actors, were reportedly detained during the raid. The youth think that drugs are cool and a creativity booster.

Youngsters often believe that drugs and alcohol can enhance creativity and seek inspiration through them. However, recent research challenges this notion and suggests that drugs and substances are not effective for any such creativity as previously believed. The romanticized idea of drugs and alcohol as a source of inspiration for artists, musicians, and writers has been challenged by a team of researchers from the University of Essex- UK, and the Humboldt University of Berlin, Germany. They found that complex training programmes, meditation, and cultural exposure are more effective methods for stimulating creativity. Their analysis of various research papers revealed that practising meditation and participating in training courses were the most successful techniques for boosting imagination and creativity. According to the study published in *Psychology of Aesthetics, Creativity, and the Arts*, training programmes that emphasize mental techniques for enhancing creativity have the most significant long-term effects. The study also found that mindfulness activities such as meditation and open thinking were effective in boosting imagination in the short term. Drugs and substance abuse have no role in boosting creativity and the message that drugs do not enhance creativity is a positive one.

Uttarakhand:
The Pharma Pills

In 2020, 1,282 NDPS cases were booked, leading to 1,449 arrests.

Uttarakhand is increasingly becoming home to a major drug problem. Uttarakhand Police busted an intra-state drug racket, seizing approximately 8008 kg of narcotic substances, and arrested two local police officers who were accomplices in drug smuggling.

Youth in various parts of the state have turned to substance abuse in recent years. Nainital has been hit the hardest. The

Nainital Police Department filed 406 cases under the NDPS Act in 2021.

The police raid revealed a drug ring that was operating out of the jail. The drug network was exposed during raids in Dehradun, Pauri, Kotdwar, and Rishikesh.

According to the data, there were 1,802 cases under the NDPS Act in 2021, with 2,104 accused arrested and drugs worth ₹26.4 crore seized. In 2020, there were 1,282 NDPS Act cases, which led to 1,449 arrests and the seizure of drugs worth ₹12.9 crore, which is almost half of what was seized the year before.

The NCB has seized 30.5 lakh Opioid pills, 70,000 CBCS, and nearly 15 kg of Amphetamine manufactured by a pharmaceutical company in Haridwar, Uttarakhand. According to the agency, the pharmaceutical company allegedly falsified records and sold the drugs to traffickers who shipped them to the United Kingdom, the United States, and Europe via the postal service. A total of 37 seizures occurred, including 22 million tramadol-like psychotropic tablets and 245 kg of psychotropic drugs.

TAMIL NADU: THE NOVEL METHODS

Three hundred and ten kilos of Ganja-laced chocolates seized.

On arrival in Tuticorin, Tamil Nadu, officials seized 300 kg of Cocaine drugs worth approximately 500 crore from a container ship arriving from Panama via Antwerp ports.

Customs officers at Chennai's Foreign Post Office (FPO) seized 46.8 kg of Kenyan khat leaves. Khat is a deciduous shrub primarily grown in East Africa and South Yemen. It contains Amphetamine-like stimulants as well as the euphoric alkaloids cathinone and cathine. Chennai Air Customs seized 15.6 kg of khat leaves worth ₹40 lakh at FPO Chennai in March 2020.

From an export shipment bound for the UAE, Chennai Customs seized 49.2 kg of Pseudoephedrine concealed within the paperboard packaging material.

In early March, Chennai Air Customs seized a package containing MDMA-containing **"blue punisher tablets"** at the FPO. This tablet contains 300 mg or more of MDMA and is three times as potent as regular Ecstasy tablets.

The police seized MDMA, Ecstasy, LSD stamps, Meth Crystals, Kush Weed, Magic Mushrooms, Ganja, and Yaba tablets, which were used as party drugs. Many drug peddlers were arrested in Chennai and Tiruvallur. Chennai police have seized 200 kg of Ganja that was smuggled into the state from Andhra Pradesh, in a recent crackdown in February 2023. In the wake of the recent seizure of Ganja-laced chocolates in Coimbatore, the police have directed private courier services to obtain a declaration from customers confirming that their parcels do not contain narcotics or Ganja. In the past two months, around 310 kg of Ganja-laced chocolates have been seized, which are believed to have been manufactured and brought mainly from Uttar Pradesh and Bihar.

UTTAR PRADESH: THE UNDISPUTED LEADER

Uttar Pradesh is the state with the highest prevalence of Cannabis use.

When it comes to drug use and trafficking in India, Uttar Pradesh ranks as one of the most worrisome states. There were more than 10,000 cases of NDPS violations in Uttar Pradesh in 2020.

Approximately two per cent (2.2 crore people approx.) were observed to use bhang, and approximately 1.2 per cent (1.3 crore people approx.) utilized illegal Cannabis products in India. Uttar Pradesh is the state with the highest prevalence of Cannabis use.

Opioids are used by 2.06 per cent of Indians. Heroin is a popular opioid (1.14 per cent). Pharmaceutical opioids (0.96 per cent) and Opium (0.52 per cent) are next. More than half of the estimated 77 million problem opioid users in the country come from a few states of which Uttar Pradesh tops the list.

In May 2022, the Gujarat ATS seized 210 kg of Heroin worth ₹775 crore and 55 kg of suspected chemicals used in the manufacture of narcotics in a follow-up action in Muzaffarnagar, Uttar Pradesh. Police seized 13.2 kg of Opium from drug traffickers in Shahjahanpur, which is worth ₹13 crore on the international market.

In Uttar Pradesh, there is legal Opium cultivation in places like Barabanki, Bareilly, Lucknow, and Faizabad. Opium diversion and illegal production are common. In these Opium fields, drug mafias have spread their tentacles.

> The price at which the government purchases Opium and the illicit market price are opposed. Farmers are enticed to divert a portion of their Opium crop to the illegal market.

Another issue is the law implementation. According to the law, the husk of the first poppy crop, also known as *dodha posht* must be destroyed before a new license is issued to the farmer. They must present the destruction certificate to the Central Bureau of Narcotics (CBN) before being granted permission to continue cropping. Nonetheless, it is reported that many times, farmers are being issued licenses despite the clear policy. These farmers then illegally sell the husk to the drug cartels. There are umpteen episodes of seizure of *dodha posht* or husk.

Rajasthan: The Border State

ISI chose the Rajasthan border to smuggle the narcotics.

Two hundred and thirty-four kilos of Opium were seized in Rajasthan. This was the country's largest Opium seizure in 2020. The Opium was sourced from the legal cultivation area of Chittorgarh and was destined for Jodhpur, according to a preliminary investigation. The latest case revealed that some legal cultivators, particularly those in Madhya Pradesh's Mandsaur, Neemuch, and Ratlam districts, and Rajasthan's Chittorgarh and Jhalawar districts, diverted Opium through illegal channels and sold it to intermediaries for financial gain.

The recent seizure of 54 kilos of Heroin from the India-Pakistan border in Bikaner, Rajasthan, has both the Border Security Force (BSF) and the NCB perplexed.

The Heroin was packed in PVC pipes, which were then pushed through a border fence near Khajuwala in the Bikaner sector, which comes under the Bundli post.

It is speculated that the ISI chose the Rajasthan border to smuggle the narcotics after striking a deal with Indian smugglers in Punjab who would send the money for the Heroin to terrorist groups in Kashmir.

Due to increased vigilance on the Punjab border, drug smugglers find it difficult to enter India. As a result, the Bikaner sector was chosen because it was close to Punjab and the goods could be easily transported.

MADHYA PRADESH: THE OPIUM ORIGIN

The NCB busted a Heroin cartel by arresting a Nigerian, an expert in enhancing the potency of narcotics through mixtures and two Mizoram women in Itarsi, Madhya Pradesh, along with 20 kg of Heroin worth ₹100 crore.

> The Indore Police seized 70 kg of MDMA drugs from five accused in a drug crackdown, one of the largest drug seizures in India.

The Anti-Terrorism Squad (ATS) arrested two people in Madhya Pradesh's Betul district for allegedly possessing Methadone worth ₹5 crore. Two gang members were apprehended, along with 20 kg of Marijuana they were selling as supernatural stevia dry leaves. In the previous seven months, 384 shipments totalling 768 kg of Marijuana were sold on online platforms to Rajasthan, Uttar Pradesh, and Madhya Pradesh. In all cases, payment was made with a single UPI ID.

About 34.6 MT of Opium-based drugs and 11.8 MT of Cannabis-based drugs were seized from Madhya Pradesh in 2019.

> More than 3100 drug abuse and trafficking cases were booked under NDPS Act in the year 2020.

The state figures in the top ten states where people have opioid and Cannabis-related problems. The CBN seized Poppy Straw weighing 3213.60 kg, concealed under a cover cargo of 62 cartons of *namkeen* in March 2023

The facts speak for themselves and have an obvious sign of the drug problem that is plaguing the state of Madhya Pradesh.

ODISHA: CANNABIS CAPITAL OF INDIA

Odisha is known as the Cannabis capital of India. The Cannabis corridor connects Odisha to northern Indian states, passing through Chhattisgarh and Madhya Pradesh. In Odisha, a whopping quantum of 61 MT of Cannabis was seized in 2019.

> Illicit Cannabis is grown in major parts of Odisha, and it is smuggled to various states, including Uttar Pradesh, Maharashtra, Telangana, and Tamil Nadu.

As of 2020, the Odisha STF has been actively combating the illegal drug trade there. Since then, the STF has seized more than 47 kg of brown sugar and apprehended 122 people suspected of trafficking illegal drugs. According to the NCRB 2020 report, the Odisha State Police under the NDPS had registered a staggering 1031 cases of drug-related crimes

In February 2023, the police in Uttar Pradesh's Greater Noida seized over 500 kg of Cannabis, which was being smuggled into the National Capital Region from Odisha's Ganjam. The total value of the seized consignment is estimated to be worth more than ₹1 crore in the market.

In Borrigumma, Odisha, the police have seized around 1,100 kg of Ganja from a pick-up van at Irrigation Colony. A novel modus operandi using an ambulance to transport drugs so that the same cannot be detected or intercepted by the police has come into the limelight.

Cultivation of Cannabis in tribal districts has burgeoned under the protection of left-wing Maoist outfits. However, as their influence dwindles, a substantial decrease in production volume is expected. Nonetheless, the Cannabis industry continues to satisfy the demand of North India. In addition, a mounting worry in the region is the escalating prevalence of Heroin. The STF intercepted over 55 kg of contraband in 2021, with an additional 23 kg already confiscated by June 2021. The drug trade is mainly focused in the coastal areas of Odisha, with Bhubaneswar serving as a prime destination.

> The significant concentration of educational institutions, including over a hundred professional colleges with over half a lakh students, has attracted the organized drug trade.

Despite concerted law enforcement efforts, the drug trade from international borders persists, flowing through West Bengal.

Jharkhand: The Illicit Opium Belt

In India, illegal Opium cultivation is primarily concentrated in Naxal-infested regions. In Jharkhand cities such as Chatra, Khunti, Ranchi, Hazaribagh, Ramgarh, Jamtara, Latehar, Palamu, and Seraikela-Kharsawan, Opium is illicitly grown on more than 5,000 acres. Preventing the cultivation of Opium on tens of thousands of acres of land annually presents a significant challenge for the state police.

> In 2021, the police destroyed the Opium crops that were illicitly growing on about 3,000 acres of land in the Jharkhand state.

The police are running a campaign in every district to get rid of the Opium crops. Sensing the gravity of the situation, the Jharkhand chief secretary recently held a video conference with the elected Panchayat Raj Institutions (PRI) representatives of 90 panchayats worst affected by poppy cultivation and sought their cooperation in combating the menace. This demonstrates the magnitude of the drug menace in Jharkhand.

This lucrative trade attracts young people from both Jharkhand and Punjab. The Opium that sells for ₹55,000 per kg on average here easily fetches more than a lakh in Punjab and other places. Around 30 drug traffickers from Punjab,

Haryana, and western Uttar Pradesh were apprehended in Jharkhand.

There has been a significant shift in consumption patterns from natural psychotropic substances to chemical compounds and a number of young people visiting party drug hotspots. 10,000 strips of Nitrosun-10, a highly intoxicating drug was recently seized. Jharkhand youths are falling victim to the rampant use of narcotic drugs in the steel city these days.

Bihar: The Toffee Ganja

A new drug has surfaced in the market—toffee laced with Ganja.

The state of Bihar plays a prominent role in the issue of narcotics trafficking and drug abuse in India. Illegal cultivation is a significant source of illicit income for certain groups in Bihar, The Red Corridor regions of Bihar have witnessed the largest seizures of narcotics, including Morphine, Heroin, and Hashish.

Moreover, a resident of Bihar was caught smuggling Nepalese Charas worth ₹2.5 crore through non-popular routes to supply various groups in Uttar Pradesh, Madhya Pradesh, Delhi, Haryana, and Punjab. Between 2015 and May 2020, the police in Bihar claimed to have seized a significant quantity of illegal drugs a total of 68,411 kg of Ganja and 951.33 kg of Charas were confiscated during this period. The DRI seized a total of 13,446 kg of Ganja in Bihar in 2020-21.

Furthermore, Hashish is transported from Nepal into India through the states of Bihar, eventually making its way to Delhi and Mumbai.

A new drug has surfaced in the market, toffee laced with Ganja.

The drug is believed to be marketed as a medicinal product and is mostly originating from the Uttar Pradesh-Bihar belt. It is being smuggled in by migrants to various parts of the country. The price per piece of Ganja chocolate may range from ₹500 to ₹1800. There have been many instances recently where Ganja-laced toffee was seized in different states. About 310 kg of Ganja-laced chocolates was seized in South India. All fingers are pointing back to the Bihar-UP belt where this new-age drug originated.

Jammu-Kashmir: The Narco War

Kashmir has surpassed Punjab in the number of drug abuse cases.

In narcotics, huge sums of money are exchanged between recipients and suppliers of drugs, as has been observed all over the world. This is missing in the narco-trade between Kashmir Valley recipients and Pakistani suppliers. Such distinctions separate the existence of narco-trade in other parts of the world from narco-terrorism in Kashmir.

Following a major crackdown by law enforcement agencies on hawala operators, Pakistan-based organizations turned to cross-LoC (Line of Control) trade and narcotics to fund terrorism and unrest in the Valley. However, since the closure of cross-border trade in early 2019, narco-trafficking appears to have become the sole means of funding terrorism and unrest.

In the year 2019, more than 24 MT of Opium-based drugs and 1 MT of Charas were seized. According to J&K police data, over 152 kg of Heroin and 49.7 kg of Brown Sugar were recovered from various parts of the state in 2020.

In 2020, the police had registered 1,132 drug trafficking cases and arrested 1672 people.

Pakistan, after selling Kashmiri youths illusions and *azadi*-inspired fantasies, is now selling them drugs.

> In February 2023, it was reported that handlers based in Pakistan were utilizing smugglers to distribute drugs in Kashmir Valley to promote drug addiction amongst the region's youth.

On the night of February 23 and 24, police announced that they had apprehended two drug smugglers and seized a significant amount of narcotics near the LoC in Kupwara district. The suspects were allegedly transporting drug shipments from across the border. In Srinagar, the issue of drug addiction has become a prevalent problem, with drug peddlers operating in Baramulla, Budgam, and Kulgam districts, specifically in the Nowpora area.

To combat drug trafficking, the District Magistrate of Shopian has implemented strict measures, including the seizure and freezing of unlawfully obtained properties. The district administration has issued notices to various individuals who have been involved in drug trafficking, requesting that they disclose any relevant information.

According to a recent study conducted by the AIIMS, Punjab has 1.2 per cent of opiate users, while Kashmir has a significantly higher percentage at 2.87 per cent.

> The Psychiatry department of the Government Medical College has recently conducted a study that has revealed that Kashmir has surpassed Punjab in the number of drug abuse cases and is currently ranked as the second-highest state in India with regard to drug abuse.

The research was conducted in all ten districts of Kashmir, and the results highlighted some alarming statistics regarding the substance-use scenario in the region.

The study further revealed that the majority of drug abusers in Kashmir were between the ages of 17 to 33 years, and unemployed youth were among the primary consumers of these drugs. Shockingly, the number of drug abusers in the valley has now surpassed 67,000, with 33,000 of them injecting Heroin using syringes, resulting in a significant increase in young deaths due to drug overdose. It was also observed that 30 to 40 per cent of addicts suffered from overdose symptoms. While Northeast India tops the list of drug abuse cases in the country, Kashmir is not far behind and has seen a significant increase in drug abuse cases.

In March 2023, the Jammu and Kashmir police dismantle a narco-terror module in Poonch, near the LoC. The operation involved the recovery of a significant amount of contraband, including 7 kg of Heroin, nearly ₹2 crore in cash, and several arms and ammunition. The seizure has brought to light a new and alarming trend, where drugs and weapons are being smuggled together from Pakistan into India. The weapons are then supplied to terrorists, while the proceeds from the drug trade are returned to handlers across the border, and a part of it is shared by local peddlers.

CHHATTISGARH: THE NAXAL GANJA

Indian insurgents rely on drug trafficking for funding, so illegal drugs are a national security issue. According to reports, Naxal groups in Odisha, Chhattisgarh, and Andhra Pradesh are using drug money to raise cadres and buy arms and ammunition. It identified the major rail routes and plugged the source of transporting drugs into various parts of the country to a large extent. The Railway Protection Force (RPF) was given powers to seize drugs and arrest people involved in smuggling under the NDPS Act on April 11, 2019. The outcomes have been fruitful. Since 2019, the RPF has arrested 1085 people and seized drugs worth over ₹27 crore under the NDPS act.

The Anti-Narcotic authorities in the Gaurela-Pendra-Marwahi district of Chhattisgarh seized Cannabis worth ₹4.5 crore in separate operations involving nine individuals.

> The confiscated drugs totalled over 32 quintals, and the individuals involved in smuggling used various methods to evade checkpoints, including travelling in luxury cars, ambulances, trucks, and even vegetable carriers.

A Ganja smuggling operation between Andhra Pradesh and Chhattisgarh was uncovered by Hyderabad police on October 22. During the operation, the police seized 1.3 tons of Ganja, with a value exceeding ₹2.8 crore, from the vehicle. To evade detection, the smugglers concealed the small Ganja packets within a load of broken rice.

In February 2020, the DRI apprehended four individuals and confiscated 2,068 kg of Ganja in two distinct incidents that took place in Raipur and Indore. In the first incident, a septic tank cleaning truck was carrying 1,230 kg of Ganja, while in the second incident, a trailer truck was found carrying 838 kg of the drug.

GOA—THE RÚSSKAYA MÁFIYA

The sun-soaked shores of Goa have become a focal point in the international drug trade.

The Indian state of Goa has seen a significant increase in drug seizures, with 156 kg of drugs worth over ₹3.60 crore being seized in the first eight months of 2022. The state government has stepped up efforts to curb the menace of substance abuse, and the governor has emphasized the government's commitment to security and safety for both citizens and tourists. Despite these efforts, Goa continues to be a hub for the drug trade and drug-related deaths continue to occur. The state has a long history of drug problems, with drugs first coming to Goa with hippies six decades ago, and now domestic tourists also falling prey to drug peddlers.

It's concerning to hear that the drug problem in Goa is still persistent, despite the government's efforts to combat it. The rising number of drug-related deaths and cases registered under the NDPS Act highlights the need for more effective measures to be taken.

Effective drug enforcement strategies typically include interdiction and seizure of illegal drugs, as well as investigation and prosecution of drug traffickers. In addition, there is a need for education and prevention programmes to raise awareness about the dangers of drug use and reduce demand for these substances.

It is also important for the government to engage with local communities, law enforcement agencies, and other stakeholders to develop a comprehensive approach to addressing the drug problem in Goa. This could include increasing resources for drug treatment and rehabilitation programmes, improving coordination between agencies, and strengthening cross-border cooperation to disrupt the supply of drugs.

The drug problem in Goa is not just a matter of law enforcement, but a complex social issue that requires a multi-faceted approach. By working together and utilizing all available resources, it is possible to make progress in reducing the harm caused by drugs in the coastal state.

> Drug trafficking and abuse is a serious problem in Goa and has been causing harm to the local communities and tourists.

Despite government efforts to implement a zero-tolerance policy and carry out surprise checks, the illegal drug trade continues to thrive. The arrest of the Nigerian national woman is just one example of the widespread drug trafficking taking place in the state.

Law enforcement agencies must take swift and effective action against drug dealers and traffickers in order to curb the illegal drug trade and reduce its harmful impact on the people of Goa. At the same time, the government needs to address the root causes of drug abuse and provide support for those struggling with addiction.

Goa, known for its sunny beaches, has become a hub for drug trafficking which has resulted in multiple drug-related deaths among visitors. Despite the government's claim of a zero-tolerance policy against drug trafficking and surprise checks in establishments, drug incidents continue to occur. A recent arrest of a Nigerian woman who attempted to smuggle drugs worth ₹15,10,000 from Delhi by train highlights the issue. Official records show an increase in cases of drug offences from 2017 to 2021.

According to recent disclosures, the notorious alleged drug lord Edwin Nunes admitted to the authorities that his suppliers were a disparate array of foreigners, ranging from Russians to individuals hailing from African nations. Further corroborating these claims, an Israeli drug dealer confirmed that he had received his stash of illicit substances from a police storage facility in Goa, which had been infiltrated and purloined by corrupt officers. Despite attempts at covering up the theft, a massive quantity of 24 kg of Hashish reportedly vanished from the anti-drug storage, with the Goa Home Minister offering the absurd explanation that the drugs had been "consumed by white ants".

> The sun-soaked shores of Goa have unfortunately become a focal point in the international drug trade, with a reputation as both a centre of consumption and distribution.

Law enforcement reports suggest that an overwhelming majority of illicit substances entering the region are brought in by foreign individuals, predominantly Russians, via chartered flights. Despite this, a significant portion of drug trafficking still occurs through maritime channels. Regrettably, Goa has also become a transit point for drugs circulating across the globe, with many transient individuals opting to stay and partake in the illicit manufacturing of synthetic drugs.

The illicit drug trade in Goa is thriving, and CK1, a dangerous combination of Cocaine and ketamine, is widely available on the North Goa beaches of Candolim, Baga, Calangute, Anjuna, Vagator, and Arambol, and sold under the false names "blizzard" and "Calvin Klein". Foreigners hold a critical place in the intricate web of relationships between politicians and drug gangs in Goa. During the early years of this decade, the drug trade in Goa was dominated by the British and Israelis. However, Nigerian individuals play a relatively minor role, serving mainly as local drug runners.

Goa sees a lot of foreign tourists, especially Russians, who are known for spending a lot of money. However, some of these tourists also get involved in illegal activities like selling drugs and online gambling. From time to time, the police catch these individuals and arrest them.

> As reports indicate, the drug trade in Goa is now largely controlled by the Rússkaya Máfiya, also known as the Russian Mafia, solidifying Russia's place as a leading force in the global drug market.

The once formidable Israeli drug networks are struggling to keep up with the overwhelming power and scale of the Russian drug empire. Thousands of affluent Russian tourists arrive in Goa each season on chartered flights, with many Kazakhstani visitors also making the journey to this popular destination.

The Russian presence in Goa is not only limited to being mere tourists but extends to the realm of commerce as well. Many Russian nationals have established restaurants in the state, which are highly sought after by foreign tourists. A local resident from the coastal belt stated that these individuals conduct their business under the guise of local proxies, who provide the premises for their operations.

The North Goa beaches, including Anjuna, Baga, Calangute, Candolim, Arambol, and Vagator, are notorious for their vibrant and extended nightlife. A vast array of beach shacks, spread across a three-kilometre stretch of sand, offer endless opportunities for pleasure-seeking revelry. The area around Anjuna Beach, in particular, is known for its high concentration of drug dealers, who flock to the area to take advantage of its massive party scene. This is also where Dr Jawaharlal Henriques, a renowned rehabilitation specialist, runs his clinic in Siolim, seeing as many as eighty to ninety patients each tourist season.

> The Goa police are still grappling with the case of Sonali Phogat, a popular Tiktok celebrity who was a victim of a drug overdose.

According to official records, in the year 2019, Goa welcomed a staggering 71,27,000 domestic tourists and 9,31,000 foreign tourists, with Russian nationals constituting a significant proportion of the latter.

> It is estimated that around 90,000 Russian tourists visit Goa each year, although the numbers have been impacted by the ongoing COVID-19 pandemic in the last three years.

In recent years, several Russian nationals have been apprehended in Goa for cultivating Marijuana within rented apartments in the beach-side villages of Anjuna and Morjim. These incidents have raised eyebrows among the local residents, who question how these tourists are able to grow such plants within the confines of their abodes. The arrests of a Russian couple in 2018, a four-member gang in 2019, and yet another individual in 2020, have shed light on the illicit activities being carried out by some foreign visitors in the coastal state.

On September 29, 2022, the Goa police apprehended a Russian national, Maxim Makarov, aged 38, for possessing 900 grams of hashish oil with an estimated value of ₹9,00,000. He was residing in Morjim at the time of his arrest. A week prior to this, on September 22, the Goa Police arrested two Russian individuals for their supposed participation in online gambling. It is believed that tourists who prolong their stays in Goa often become embroiled in these illicit trades after they develop close relationships with locals and become familiar with the area. In May 2023, three individuals were arrested in Goa by the NCB for their alleged involvement in an "international drug cartel". Among them was a former Russian police officer who was identified as the leader of the operation. The other two individuals included an Indian accomplice and a person who had previously won a silver medal in swimming at the 1980 Olympics.

To carry out this illegal activity, they blend in with the tourist crowd and often go unnoticed. However, local authorities have been vigilant in cracking down on such individuals, leading to several arrests over the years. Despite these efforts, the drug trade remains a persistent problem, with some tourists continuing to engage in this illegal activity.

Section 2

An Eye Opener

A Calendar of Drug Seizures—The Timeline

The crime rate, which measures the number of crimes per 100,000 people, is reported by the National Crime Records Bureau (NCRB). Their latest release for the year 2021 provides detailed state-wise data on Narcotic cases and Crime rates, revealing the severity of the drug issue in different parts of the country.

Punjab records the highest crime rate, with Himachal Pradesh and the Northeast States following closely behind. Kerala and Jammu Kashmir also have significantly higher crime rates than the national average.

The quantity of drugs seized in a particular state can be an indicator of the volume of drugs being trafficked into and out of that state. Among the most widely abused drugs are Opium-based and Cannabis-based drugs. These two drug types are often seized in large quantities by law enforcement agencies.

Several Indian states reported significant seizures of Opium-based drugs in the year 2021.

Rajasthan seized the highest amount, with over 124,000 kg of Opium-based drugs, including Poppy Husk.

Jharkhand seized more than 16,000 kg, while Punjab and Madhya Pradesh reported seizures of over 35,000 kg and 37,000 kg respectively. Haryana also recorded a seizure of over 8,000 kg of Opium-based drugs, including Poppy Husk. In Jammu and Kashmir, the seizure of Opium-based drugs, including Poppy Husk, was more than 19,500 kg in the year 2021. These seizures highlight the significant challenge posed by the trafficking and consumption of Opium-based drugs in India.

In the year 2021, Andhra Pradesh recorded the seizure of more than 1,90,000 kg of Cannabis-based drugs, including Ganja.

In Odisha, the seizure was 169,000 kg, while Uttar Pradesh reported a seizure of more than 100 MT of the same. Bihar had a seizure of more than 27,000 kg of Cannabis-based drugs including ganja, and West Bengal recorded a seizure of more than 27,000 kg as well. In Chhattisgarh, the seizure of Cannabis-based drugs, including Ganja, was more than 27,500 kg in the same year. Apart from these drugs, hundreds of kilos of different drugs like Cocaine, Heroin, and party drugs like Ecstasy pills/MDMA drugs, Yaba, Mephedrone, and Methamphetamines are smuggled into the country. Where just a few grams of these drugs cost thousands of rupees, one can imagine the magnitude of money tangled and illegal funds involved.

There are millions of drug addicts throughout India today, and the nation is rapidly becoming a major drug-consuming hotspot.

The high number of seizures of these drugs across various states of India may be encouraging for drug enforcement agencies but at the same time highlights the widespread use and abuse of drugs in the country.

A glance at the drug seizures across the country around the year gives an insight into the growing menace. It is pertinent to note that the following figures are just illustrative and not exhaustive.

Feb 13, 2022

- 234 kg of Crystal Methamphetamine drugs and 529 kg of Hashish, worth ₹2000 crore seized off the Gujarat coast

Feb 19, 2022

- 4.58 kg Ecstasy pills/MDMA drugs pills worth ₹ 9.82 crore seized at the international airport in Bengaluru

March 29, 2022

- 14 kg opium seized at Auriya, Uttar Pradesh

March 31, 2022

- 02.945 kg of Heroin seized at Amritsar
- 12.5 kg Opium seized at Ajmer, destined for Bihar

April 6, 2022

- 4601.78 kg of Ganja seized at Agartala, destined for Bihar
- 5.19 kg seized at IGI Airport, Delhi

- 10,000 tramadol tablets seized at Ludhiana, Punjab
- 03.035 kg seized at HQ Srikaranpur, Jodhpur

April 9, 2022

- 150 kg Poppy Husk seized at Ahmedabad, Gujarat
- 2.3 kg Charas seized at Amritsar, Punjab
- 168 gm Mephedrone seized at Ahmedabad

April 12, 2022

- 41.035 kg Ganja seized at Kolkata
- 1.34 kg Cocaine seized at IGI Airport Delhi
- 4.956 kg of Pseudoephedrine seized at Hyderabad
- 538 kg of Ganja seized at Bokaro, Jharkhand
- 1.290 kg Opium seized at Haryana
- 3.05 kg Heroin seized at Sri Ganganagar, Jodhpur

April 14, 2022

- Heroin worth ₹24 crore seized at Mumbai
- 69 kg of Ganja seized at Narsingpur, Madhya Pradesh
- 3.980 kg of Heroin seized at Mumbai Airport

April 15, 2022

- 508 gms of tramadol seized at Andheri Mumbai
- 155.5 kg Poppy Straw seized at Kishangarh, Bhilwara, Rajasthan

April 24, 2022

- 184 gms of Methamphetamine seized at Chennai Airport

April 25, 2022

- 5.3 kg of Opium seized in Manipur

April 27, 2022

- 35 kg Heroin seized in Gujarat
- 2400 kg (2.4 MT) Ganja seized in Odisha

April 30, 2022

- Heroin worth ₹ 450 crore was seized at Pipavav Port, Gujarat

May 6, 2022

- 3.2 kg Heroin seized in Rajasthan
- 506 kg of Ganja seized in Amrapali, Odisha

May 13, 2022

- 4.780 kg Charas seized in Chandigarh

May 15, 2022

- 1.770 kg of Hydroponic Weed worth ₹ 1.5 crore was seized in Mumbai

May 19, 2022

- 204 kg Ganja seized in Berhampur, Odisha

May 22, 2022

- 28.694 kg Opium seized in Assam

May 23, 2022

- 2.25 kg Pseudoephedrine seized in Chennai
- 885.150 kg of Ganja seized from Sonepur, Odisha
- 8640 bottles of CBCS were seized in Mumbai.
- 970 gms Amphetamine seized at Mumbai
- 645.88kg Ganja seized at Tripura

May 24, 2022

- 426.910 kg Ganja seized in Guwahati, Assam

May 26, 2022

- Cocaine worth ₹ 500 crore was seized near Mundra Port, Gujarat.

May 27, 2022

- 620 grams of Heroin and 2.58 kg of Brown Sugar were seized from Ghazipur, Patna.
- 2.93kg Ephedrine seized from Chennai

May 28, 2022

- 34.89 kg of Heroin was seized in pan-India raids in New Delhi, Mumbai, and Bangalore.
- 970 grams of Amphetamine seized in Mumbai.
- 14.7 kg Opium seized at the Haryana-Punjab border
- 750 gm Heroin seized at New Delhi

June 3, 2022

- 1191.2 kg Ganja seized at Manipur
- 0.825 kg of Heroin seized at the Manipur-Myanmar border
- 5 kg Opium seized at Bikaner, Rajasthan

June 4, 2022

- 535 gm (49 capsules) of Heroin and 175 gm (15 capsules) of Cocaine were seized at Mumbai

June 5, 2022

- 3.5 kg Heroin seized at Delhi

- 1010 kg Marijuana seized at Odisha
- 68 kg alprazolam/nordazepam seized at Vapi, Gujarat
- 16.777 kg Heroin was seized at Guwahati, Assam

June 7, 2022

- 3.6 kg Heroin worth ₹ 17 crore was seized in Rajasthan.

June 8, 2022

- 20,000 bottles of CBCS seized at Murshidabad, Kolkata
- 1,200 bottles of CBCS seized at Bihar

June 11, 2022

- 523 kg Ganja seized at Surat, Gujarat

June 12, 2022

- 4.880 kg Hashish seized at Mumbai
- 1582 kg of Ganja seized at Cooch Behar, Kolkata

June 13, 2022

- 490 gms Methamphetamine and 435 gms Amphetamine seized at Mumbai
- 290 gm Heroin seized at Moreh, Manipur
- 4.88 kg of Charas seized at Mumbai

June 15, 2022

- 1.350 kg of Opium and 17 kg of Ganja seized at Cooch Behar, Kolkata

June 18, 2022

- 724 kg Ganja worth ₹ 1.45 crore seized at Surat, Gujarat

- 348 gm of Morphine seized at Lucknow
- 352 kg of Ganja seized at Ahmedabad

June 19, 2022

- 348 gm of Heroin seized at Barabanki, Uttar Pradesh
- 3.62 kg of Charas seized at Kullu, Himachal Pradesh

June 23, 2022

- 141 kg of Ganja seized at Indore, Madhya Pradesh
- 1484.95 kg Ganja seized at Guwahati, destined for Bihar

July 10, 2022

- 297.52 kg Ganja seized at Bihar
- 4.1 kg Opium, 194.2 kg Poppy Straw, and 600 tabs of diphenoxylate HCL seized at Punjab
- 1728.90 kg Ganja seized at Tripura

July 13, 2022

- Heroin worth ₹ 350 crore seized at Mundra Port, Gujarat

July 15, 2022

- 73 kg of Heroin worth ₹730 crore at Nhava Sheva Port, Mumbai

July 27, 2022

- 60 kg of Cannabis seized in Rameswaram, Tamil Nadu

August 2, 2022

- 273 packets of Cannabis washed ashore off the Saurashtra coast in Gujarat.

- 363 packets of Cannabis 1 also washed ashore off the Saurashtra coast in Gujarat.

August 3, 2022

- 1.939 kg of Brown Sugar valued at ₹1.94 crore seized from Manipur

August 16, 2022

- Mephedrone valued at ₹1026 crore seized in Gujarat by Mumbai ATS

August 18, 2022

- 225 kg of Mephedrone valued at ₹ 1125 crore seized in Gujarat

September 3, 2022

- 210 kg high-grade Ganja seized at Mumbai
- 10.8 kg of Charas seized at Gorakhpur, Uttar Pradesh

September 6, 2022

- 210 kg Ganja worth ₹4 crore seized at Raigad, Maharashtra

September 9, 2022

- 185 gms Ephedrine seized at Mumbai

September 8, 2022

- 337 kg of Ganja seized at Tripura

September 9, 2022

- 39.5 kg of Heroin worth ₹ 200 crore seized at Kolkata Port

September 10, 2022

- 307.150 kg Poppy Straw seized at Jodhpur

September 12, 2022

- 908.70 kg Ganja value at ₹ 1.36 crore seized at Tripura

September 14, 2022

- 40 kg of Heroin, Jakhau in Gujarat

September 16, 2022

- 345 kg of Heroin at JNPT, Mumbai

September 23, 2022

- Seized 2086 gms Heroin valued at ₹ 4.17 crore seized at Manipur

September 29, 2022

- 3.2 kg Black Cocaine seized at Cuttack

October 1, 2022

- 198 kg of Methamphetamines and 9 kg of Cocaine, Navi Mumbai

October 6, 2022

- 50 kg of Cocaine worth ₹500 crore from Nava Sheva, Mumbai

October 8, 2022

- 200 kg of Heroin worth ₹1,200 crore from Kochi, off Kerala Coast

- 50 kg of Heroin worth ₹350 crore from the mid-sea, off Gujarat Coast

October 9, 2022

- 60,000 Amphetamine/Yaba tablets valued at ₹6 crore seized in Bishnupur District, Manipur

October 19, 2022

- 50,000 Amphetamine/Yaba tablets value seized at ₹ 5 crore in Thoubal District, Manipur

October 20, 2022

- 4.729 kg of Methaqualone worth ₹2.36 crore seized at Chennai Airport

November 2, 2022

- 4000 gms of Heroin valued at ₹30 crore seized at IGI Airport New Delhi

November 30, 2022

- 63 kg of Mephedrone-MD drugs and raw material value at ₹478 crore seized at Vadodara, Gujarat

December 3, 2022

- 732gms of Cocaine valued at ₹11 crore seized by air customs at IGIA
- Hydro Ganja worth ₹15 lakh seized at Bengaluru

December 14, 2022

- 80 kg Ganja (Cannabis) seized at Shillong near the Indo-Bangladesh border

December 20, 2022

- 1542 gm Methaqualone and 644 gm Heroin valued at ₹5.35 crore seized at Chennai Airport
- Heroin worth ₹400 crore seized off Gujarat Coast, mid-sea

December 22, 2022

- 17,000 nos. of Yaba tablets valued at ₹1.70 crore seized in Cachar District, Assam

December 24, 2022

- 20.326 kg of Heroin seized at Ludhiana

December 29, 2022

- 4 kg Charas seized at Mumbai
- 2.064 kg Heroin seized at Banswara, Rajasthan
- 641.87 kg Ganja seized at Tripura
- 500 gm Heroin seized at Chandigarh

January 17, 2023

- 7.59 lakh tablets of Yaba tablets worth ₹40 crore

January 23, 2023

- 315.05 kg Poppy Straw seized at Mandsaur, MP

February 16, 2023

- 570 kg Ganja seized at Tripura

March 7, 2023

- 61 kg of Heroin worth ₹425 crore mid-sea near Gujarat

An Eye Opener: Stark Reality

The Ministry of Social Justice and Empowerment released a report on the "National Survey on Extent and Pattern of Substance Use in India" (2019), which shows that a significant proportion of people in India are using various types of substances. According to the report, 3.1 crore individuals or 2.8 per cent of the population use Cannabis, with 72 lakh people or 0.66 per cent of the population suffering from Cannabis-related problems. The report also reveals that 2.06 per cent of the population or an estimated number of individuals use opioids, and around 60 lakh are opioid dependent. It is worth noting that these figures were calculated based on a population of 110 crore, and with the current population of 140 crore, the numbers may have increased proportionally while keeping the same percentage as reported in the 2019 report. Hence, if the current population is factored in, the report suggests that approximately 3.92 crore individuals (2.8 per cent of the current population) use Cannabis, and 92.4 lakh people or 0.66 per cent of the population suffer from Cannabis-related problems. Additionally, an estimated 2.88 crore people or 2.06 per cent of the current population use opioids, with around 77 lakh of them suffering from opioid-related problems.

> There are almost 1.694 crore persons who are suffering from drug-related problems and are dependent, in other words, they are tempted to consume everyday drugs like Cannabis-based products like Ganja (Weed, Marijuana), Hashish, Charas or Opioid-based products viz. Hafeem, Morphine, Poppy Husk (*dodha posht*), Heroin, Smack, Brown sugar, and Chitta.

The quantity of such drugs depends on two factors, firstly the type of drug and secondly the magnitude of the drug dependency a drug addict is facing. Let us assume a very modest quantity of drugs of just 0.5 grams is consumed by them on a daily basis keeping in view that a normal cigarette weighs around one gram.

If 1.694 crore drug-dependent persons consume and abuse even 0.5 grams of drugs every day, they would consume 23.91 metric tons of drugs per week, which is 95.65 metric tons of drugs per month, and a staggering 1162.42 metric tons of drugs per year.

Here are the calculations with explanations:

One crore is equivalent to 10 million. Therefore, 1.694 crore is equivalent to:

1.694 crore = 1.694 x 10 million = 16.94 million

If a person uses 0.5 grams of drugs every day, then in a week, they would use 3.5 grams of drugs.

Therefore, the total amount of drugs needed for 16.94 million people using 0.5 grams of drugs every day for a week is:

16.94 million x 3.5 grams = 59.29 million grams

A million grams is equivalent to one metric ton.

This is equivalent to 59.29 metric tons of drugs per week.

To calculate the amount of drugs needed in a month, we can use the same formula as before:

16.94 million x 15 grams = 254.1 million grams of drugs

This is equivalent to 254.1 metric tons of drugs per month.

To calculate the number of drugs needed in a year to satisfy the needs of the drug dependent addicts, we can use the same formula as before:

16.94 million x 182.5 grams = 3,091.55 million grams of drugs

This is equivalent to 3,091 metric tons of drugs per year.

So if 1.694 crore (16.94 million) drug addicts use just a small quantity of a mere 0.5 grams of drugs every day, they would need 59.29 metric tons of drugs per week, 254 metric tons of drugs per month, and about **3,091** metric tons of drugs per year to meet their drugs consumption needs.

Moreover, there are the remaining 5.11 crore (those who use drugs but are still not totally dependent on drugs and are not drug addicts in a true sense) individuals who if they consume just 0.5 grams (a modest assumption) of drugs once a week, they would consume 25.55 metric tons of drugs per week, 102.2 metric tons of drugs per month, and 1,238.9 metric tons of drugs per year.

Here are the calculations with explanations:

One crore is equivalent to 10 million. Therefore, 5.11 crore is equivalent to:

5.11 crore = 5.11 x 10 million = 51.1 million

If one person uses 0.5 grams of drugs every week, then in a week (7 days), they would use 0.5 grams of drugs.

Therefore, the total amount of drugs needed for 51.1 million people using 0.5 grams of drugs every week is:

51.1 million x 0.5 grams = 25.55 million grams of drugs

This is equivalent to 25.55 metric tons of drugs per week.

To calculate the quantity of drugs needed in a month, we can multiply the amount of drugs needed in a week by the number of weeks in a month, which is approximately 4.3:

25.55 metric tons x 4.3 = 109.87 metric tons of drugs per month

To calculate the amount of drugs needed in a year, we can multiply the quantity of drugs needed a week by the number of weeks in a year, which is 52:

25.55 metric tons x 52 = 1,328.6 metric tons of drugs per year

3,091 metric tons + 1,328.6 metric tons is a whopping 4420 MT

It's shocking to realize that approximately **4420 MT** of illicit drugs, including both Cannabis-based and opioid-based drugs, are consumed annually in the country.

For a common man to visualize the said quantity of drugs, it is almost 442 truckloads of drugs consumed in a year.

This simple calculation is truly an eye-opener for all and highlights the alarming scale of drug abuse in the country.

The staggering amounts of illegal drugs may seem unbelievable to some. Given the enormous quantities consumed and abused by drug users each year, it's understandable that doubt would arise. The enormity of the quantities of illegal drugs may cause disbelief in some individuals. The sheer volume of consumption and abuse by drug users each year could understandably lead to doubt in anybody's mind. However, let's see an alternative perspective which can be found in a recently published report by the NCRB, under the Ministry of Home Affairs. In August 2022, the NCRB released "Crime in India – 2021," a comprehensive report containing statistics and data on various crimes committed in the country.

In the said report, Table 20B.3 gives details of seizures under NDPS Act in the year 2021 by the state/UT police. Accordingly, opium-based drugs accounted for a total of 333,312 kg of seized drugs.

Opium itself accounted for 17,438 kg, while Morphine and Heroin accounted for 46.673 kg and 68,219 kg, respectively. Within the Heroin category, Heroin and Smack accounted for 67,056 kg and 1,163 kg, respectively. Poppy Husk seizures totalled 247,607 kg.

> Further, as per the said table, Cannabis-based drugs seized totalled 796,080 kg, with Ganja making up the vast majority at 777,082 kg.

Of the Ganja seized, 768,579 kg were classified as Ganja, 8,440 kg were classified as bhang, and 61.715 kg were classified as Sulfa. Hashish seizures totalled 108.881 kg, while Charas seizures totalled 18,889 kg.

In other words, as per the said report, in the year 2021, 333 MT of Opium-based drugs were seized and 796 MT of Cannabis-based drugs were seized, a total of 1129 MT of just these drugs were seized by the state/UT police in various states and union territories.

Apart from the above, the said report also published the details of narcotic drugs seized by various other premier agencies like NCB, DRI, Customs, BSF, and other such agencies.

> In a recent report, it is claimed that between 2014 and 2022 over 62.60 lakh kg of drugs worth ₹97,000 crore were seized by various agencies in the country.

No agency in the world has ever achieved a 100 per cent success rate in preventing the production and confiscation of every gram of narcotic drug, despite their best efforts. In light of the fact that the police have seized over **1129 metric tons** of such drugs in a year, it becomes apparent that approximately 4420 metric tons of illegal drugs, including Cannabis and opioid-based substances, could potentially be consumed and abused every year. This also indicates that, regardless of the state and central drug enforcement agencies' best efforts, a significant quantity of these drugs still enters the market.

The disclosure of these facts may prompt a re-evaluation of the approach to tackle the escalating drug menace in the country, which, if left unaddressed, could have severe repercussions on future generations. It is crucial to reconsider the strategy for fighting the ongoing war on drugs, as these figures demonstrate the scale of the challenge we are facing. A new strategy that incorporates innovative approaches, in addition to the existing methods, is necessary to tackle this issue effectively.

Demystifying Drugs: Types and Effects

DRUGS OF ABUSE: NARCOTIC DRUGS CLASSES AND ABUSE

The word "narcotic" or "opioids" means drugs that make you feel less pain and less aware of what's happening around you. It comes from a Greek word that means feeling sleepy and not being able to think clearly.

Mood, thinking, and sensation alteration, pain relief, anxiety reduction, and euphoria-eliciting effects are all common goals for drug abusers. Understanding the many types of drug abuse and how they differ, and their effects is essential to comprehending their socio-economic implications.

When someone uses drugs repeatedly, their body can become physically dependent on the drug. This means that if they stop using the drug, they can experience withdrawal symptoms that can range from mild discomfort to life-threatening. These symptoms depend on how much and how the drug was used.

Physical dependence usually goes away within a few weeks after stopping drug use.

However, psychological dependence can last much longer and can be a reason why people start using drugs again after they've stopped.

This is called a relapse. People with a substance use disorder will keep using drugs even if it causes them serious problems with their health or relationships.

When we talk about narcotics, we usually think of two types: those that come from plants (plant-based) and those that are made in a laboratory (synthetic drugs). But there's a third type, called a hybrid, which is a mix of both plant and lab-made substances.

Drugs of abuse can also be classified into different categories based on their effects on humans. There are five main types of drugs: narcotics, depressants, stimulants, hallucinogens, and anabolic steroids. Narcotics are used for pain relief and can cause feelings of drowsiness or euphoria. Depressants slow down the central nervous system, leading to relaxation or sedation. Stimulants speed up the central nervous system, resulting in increased alertness, energy, and focus. Hallucinogens alter perception and can cause hallucinations or changes in mood and thought patterns. Anabolic steroids mimic the effects of testosterone, promoting muscle growth and physical performance.

Cannabis-based drugs, such as ganja, Marijuana, Weed, Charas, and Hashish, are the most abused narcotic drugs both globally and in India. Opioid-based drugs, including Opium, Morphine, Heroin, Smack, Brown Sugar, and Chitta follow closely as the second most commonly abused narcotic drug. This is followed by, Cocaine and an array of synthetic drugs like Amphetamines, MDMA, Meth, Crystal, Yaba, etc. In addition, prescription drugs are also abused in India and globally.

Cannabis-Based Drugs

Marijuana

Marijuana, also known as Ganja, Weed, or Grass, is a type of psychoactive substance derived from the Cannabis sativa plant. With almost 480 distinct components, THC (delta-9-tetrahydrocannabinol) is the primary compound responsible for the psychoactive effects of Marijuana. Typically, Marijuana is a dried, shredded mixture of Cannabis sativa flowers, stalks, seeds, and leaves. The mixture often appears green, brown, or grey and has a texture that is similar to tobacco.

> Illicit cultivation of Ganja is widespread in India, and law enforcement agencies seize tons of it every year.

Several Indian states, including Andhra Pradesh, Odisha, Uttar Pradesh, Bihar, West Bengal, and Chhattisgarh, reported significant seizures of Cannabis-based drugs, including ganja, in the year 2021. Andhra Pradesh recorded a seizure of over 190 MT, Odisha seized 169 MT, Uttar Pradesh reported more than 100 MT, while Bihar, Chhattisgarh and West Bengal all seized over 27 MT.

In contrast, Marijuana is legally cultivated in countries such as the United States, Canada, Thailand, and others.

> The legalization of Marijuana for recreational use in several countries has become a topic of heated debate.

Although it typically grows wild, Marijuana is now being cultivated in some locations across the world. Street names for Marijuana include Weed, Ganja, Grass, Blunts, Boom, Chronic, Dope, Gangster, Hash, Herb, Hydro, Indo, Joint, Mary Jane, Pot, Reefer, Sinsemilla, and Skunk.

Marijuana Consumption

Smoke Joint

Marijuana is typically smoked as a joint or through a pipe or bong. It can also be smoked in blunts, which are cigars filled with Marijuana and sometimes other drugs. Marijuana can also be ingested by blending it into food or making it into tea.

Weed Cakes and Chocolates

Marijuana is sometimes sold under the guise of herbal cigarettes, as well as being mixed into edibles like chocolate and cakes.

> Recently, Weed cakes and Weed pot brownies were seized from a bakery in Malad, Mumbai.

There have been many instances recently where Ganja-laced chocolates were seized in different states.

Marijuana Concentrates

Marijuana Concentrates are highly concentrated forms of THC that have up to four times the amount of THC found in high-grade Marijuana. THC levels could range from 40 to 80 per cent. They can be made using various techniques, including the dangerous butane extraction process. Common street names for Marijuana concentrates include honey oil, wax, shatter, and dabs. They have a visual resemblance to honey or butter and come in shades of brown or gold.

Incidents of seizures of highly concentrated THC smuggled from the USA are frequently reported. Users typically smoke them through water or oil pipes or inhale them using e-cigarettes or vaporizers, which are smokeless and easy to hide. Inhaling Marijuana concentrates through e-cigarettes or vaporizers is commonly known as "dabbing" or "vaping".

Hydroponic Weed

Hydroponics is a plant cultivation method that utilizes a water-based nutrient solution instead of soil. In the United States, a significant number of licensed Cannabis growers have adopted this advanced technique. The illicit drug dealers seem to have learned the said technique.

> In recent times, law enforcement agencies have seized Hydroponic Weed in different parts of the country.

For instance, two individuals were recently apprehended in Dombilvili, a suburb of Mumbai, for growing Cannabis through hydroponic methods. Their setup involved water pumps, air circulation systems, and photosynthesis lighting systems. Similarly, in the Satara Hills of Maharashtra, two Germans were caught cultivating Cannabis in a bungalow using hydroponic methods.

Idukki Gold

Idukki Gold, also known as Kerala Gold, is a Cannabis strain that originates from Idukki, a district in the southern Indian state of Kerala. This particular strain has gained international recognition and is highly regarded as one of the best Cannabis strains in all of Asia.

Effects of Marijuana on the body and mind

Short-term effects of Marijuana use include altered vision, impaired thinking and problem-solving abilities, and decreased coordination. Long-term use can lead to physical and psychological dependence, withdrawal symptoms, sedation, bloodshot eyes, increased heart rate, coughing, increased appetite, and increased blood pressure. Chronic Marijuana use can cause health problems such as bronchitis, emphysema, and bronchial asthma. Withdrawal from high doses of Marijuana can cause headaches, shakiness, sweating, stomach pains, and nausea.

Charas – Hashish

Hashish and Charas are two distinct forms of Cannabis products that vary in their physical form and preparation methods. Hashish is derived from the resin of the Cannabis plant, which is extracted by sifting the plant material through a fine sieve or mesh bag to collect the resinous trichomes. The collected resin is then compressed into a solid block or ball, which can be soft or hard depending on the quality of the resin and the pressing method used. Typically, Hashish is smoked in a pipe or cigarette, or mixed with other herbs or tobacco. Sulfa is also smoked as it is a variant of Charas.

In contrast, Charas is produced by rubbing fresh Cannabis leaves and buds with the hands or through a sieve, which results in the resin sticking to the skin or mesh. The collected resin is then rolled into balls or sticks, which are typically soft and pliable and range in colour from light brown to black. Charas is often smoked in a chillum or mixed with other herbs and tobacco.

To summarize, although both Hashish and Charas are made from the Cannabis plant's resin, Hashish is created by sifting and compressing the resin into a solid form, while Charas is produced by rubbing the resin from the plant material and rolling it into balls or sticks.

Hash Oil

Hashish oil, also known as Hash oil, Liquid hash, or Cannabis oil, is created by extracting cannabinoids from plant material using a solvent. The characteristics of the resulting extract, including its colour and odour, are influenced by the type of solvent used in the process. It is worth noting that just a drop or two of this liquid on a cigarette is equivalent to smoking a Marijuana joint.

Malana Cream

Malana cream is a type of high-quality Charas that is produced in Kullu Valley, Himachal Pradesh through illegal Cannabis cultivation. The region is famous for its Cannabis farming, and this particular strain is created by hand-rubbing the resin from one of the finest Cannabis plants.

It is believed that Malana Cream is sold at a premium price in Amsterdam's cafes, attracting many Cannabis enthusiasts from around the world.

Bhang

India unlike other nations has a different stand on bhang, though the same is a Cannabis-based drug. Bhang has been in use since ancient days in the country. It is made from the leaves and seeds of the Cannabis plant and thus it is not considered illegal under the NDPS Act of 1985. However, different states have their own regulations and restrictions regarding the sale and use of bhang. It is more of a state subject. In February 2017,

> Gujarat legalized bhang by removing it from the list of "intoxicating drugs" covered by section 23 of the Gujarat Prohibition Act, however, similar to many other states, certain regulations and restrictions are in place.

It is also used as *'prasad'* in Shiva temples. In a recent study, it was reported that more than two crore people in India use bhang. Almost 8000 kg of bhang was seized in 2021.

Opioid-Based Drugs

Opium

The Opium poppy, scientifically known as Papaver somniferous, is a plant that serves as the primary source of Opium—a highly addictive, non-synthetic opioid. Morphine, Codeine, and Heroin are just a few of the drugs that originate from this plant. Opium is produced by manually scraping and air-drying the milky fluid resin that seeps from the unripe seedpod of the Opium poppy. It can come in various forms, such as liquid, solid, or powder, but the fine brownish powder is the most widely available.

> Poppy cultivation is strictly regulated and authorized for medical purposes in only a few countries worldwide, and India is one of them.

It is legally cultivated in the states of Rajasthan, Uttar Pradesh, and Madhya Pradesh. In contrast, Afghanistan is the largest global producer of Opium and is considered the epicentre of the drug trade.

> Opium is commonly referred to as *hafeem* in the local language.

While the traditional method of manually extracting Opium from the milky fluid of the unripe seedpod is still in use, a more modern approach involves the industrial Poppy Straw process. This method involves extracting alkaloids from the mature dried plant, resulting in a concentrate of Poppy Straw that is used for pharmaceutical purposes. However, India continues to employ the traditional method.

Furthermore, despite legal and regulated poppy cultivation in India, there is a widespread problem of illicit poppy cultivation. Law enforcement agencies frequently attempt to eradicate these illicit crops, as it is believed that hundreds of acres of poppy are being illegally grown in the Northeastern states of the country. Additionally, there have been instances of Opium pilferage and smuggling from authorized cultivation sites.

In 2021 alone, various state police forces seized over 17 metric tons of illicit Opium. This serves as a testament to the scale of the problem and highlights the ongoing challenges faced in tackling the illegal cultivation and distribution of Opium in the country.

Opium abuse is prevalent in rural areas, where it is often consumed by smoking or ingestion. However, the abuse of this drug can lead to severe health consequences, including overdose. Symptoms of an Opium overdose may include slowed breathing, convulsions, disorientation, and weakness.

Morphine

Morphine is a narcotic that is derived from Opium, and it is an effective pain management medication that is commonly used to treat severe pain however it has a high potential for abuse.

Heroin

Heroin is made from Morphine, which comes from a poppy plant. Heroin is a dangerous and addictive drug. It's usually sold as a white or brown powder. Heroin was originally created as a pain medication by Bayer, a large pharmaceutical corporation. Today, it is only used as an illegal drug. Heroin is extremely addictive and can cause serious harm to the body. The drug is often mixed with other substances, which can change its colour and has many names, including Brown, gear, H, Horse, and Smack. Afghanistan is the world's largest producer of this drug.

Heroin is abused in various ways, such as injection, smoking, or inhalation/nasal spray. Snorting or smoking high-quality Heroin is the most common method. Due to its quick effect on the brain, Heroin is both mentally and physically addictive. The drug abuser experiences a feeling of euphoria, known as a "rush" that lasts for hours, followed by sleepiness and alertness.

Drug addicts often smoke Heroin by heating it on a surface like tin foil and inhaling the smoke. This method, known as "chasing the dragon," produces effects within a few minutes.

Heroin overdoses are prevalent, and it is responsible for more deaths than any other illegal narcotic worldwide.

If a person takes too much Heroin, they may feel drowsy. Breathing may slow down, and the person may slip into a coma. If the breathing slows down too much, the person may die.

Heroin is often mixed with other substances like sugar, starch, powdered milk, quinine, or paracetamol to increase the drug dealer's profits. This practice is known to increase the weight of the drug, making it more profitable for the seller.

In recent years, India has seen a significant increase in the smuggling of Heroin through coastal regions by drug traffickers from Pakistan, Afghanistan, and Iran.

Large quantities of Heroin have been seized as a result.

Chitta

"Chitta" in Punjabi means white colour. It is an adulterated Heroin which is one of the most abused drugs in Punjab, Himachal Pradesh, and Haryana.

Chitta is smuggled across the Pakistan-Punjab border through drones. In the past few years, the incidents of drone dropping chitta has risen exponentially.

Poppy Husk

Poppy Husk refers to the dried stalk of the poppy plant and is commonly known as *dodha posht* in the local language.

Unfortunately, it has become one of the most widely abused drugs in rural areas of Rajasthan, Madhya Pradesh, Uttar Pradesh, and Punjab. Alarming statistics from a government report in 2021 revealed that more than 247 MT of Poppy Husk was seized, highlighting the severity of the problem and the extent of its prevalence across the country.

Cocaine

Cocaine, a potent stimulant with a high potential for addiction, is derived from the leaves of the coca plant, which are typically harvested in Bolivia, Peru, and Colombia. The process of Cocaine production involves a series of chemical syntheses that take place in secluded jungle laboratories.

Mexico is currently considered the world's Cocaine capital, responsible for producing over 90 per cent of the Cocaine powder that is trafficked globally. This illicit substance is commonly known by various street names, including Blow, Coca-Cola, Coke, Crack, Flake, Snow, and Soda Cot.

Cocaine is classified into three different types: Coke, Crack, and Freebase, each with its own unique appearance. Coke, which is the most commonly used type, appears as a fine white powder. Crack, on the other hand, typically looks like small lumps or rocks, while Freebase resembles crystallized powder.

Cocaine is often sold as a white crystalline powder, but it is frequently "cut" with other substances to increase the quantity of product available and maximize dealer profits. The most common substances used to dilute or cut Cocaine are sugars and local anaesthetics.

In India, it is smuggled and abused by rich brats at rave parties, as it is very expensive when compared to other drugs. The street price of one kg is more than seven crore.

Khat

Khat is a stimulant-containing leafy green herb. Khat is a leafy green plant that contains two major stimulant chemicals that increase the pace of your mind and body. Their primary effects are comparable to, but less potent than, Amphetamine (Speed). Khat is mostly utilized in Northeast Africa and the Arabian Peninsula, however, recently, it has been believed to be smuggled in India by the Nigerian African drug cartel and abused by many.

In March 2023, the police in Pune conducted a drug bust and seized 8.4 kg of Catha edulis (Khat), a stimulant drug, from a Yemeni national who was selling it to foreign nationals in the city. The man was arrested, and the investigation revealed that he acquired the drug from people who came to India from Yemen for medical treatment. The drug is openly consumed in some African countries as well as in Yemen and acts as a stimulant, resulting in euphoria and loss of appetite.

Khat is a stimulant and chewing it can cause people to become more awake and chattier, induce feelings of elation, suppress the appetite, contribute to spells of insomnia, and produce a sensation of serenity if eaten for a few hours, with some characterizing it as being 'blissed out'. It can exacerbate pre-existing mental health issues and create delusional and psychotic behaviours which may be associated with irritability, anxiety and losing touch with reality.

Synthetic Drugs

India is experiencing a sudden surge in synthetic drugs.

The production of synthetic drugs is not limited by geography and can occur in any location based on the availability of certain chemicals and human ingenuity. As the synthetic drug market is constantly changing, it requires adaptable and quick solutions. Unlike plant-based drugs like Cocaine and Heroin, which have geographic limitations, synthetic drug manufacturing can happen anywhere.

> India is experiencing a sudden surge in synthetic drugs.

The drug mafias and drug traffickers find novel ways to smuggle these drugs into the country, through road, air, or water. Moreover, there are hundreds of makeshift clandestine labs involved in manufacturing such chemical-based drugs. The drug enforcement agencies of the state as well as the centre have busted many in the recent past.

The last decade saw a significant increase in synthetic drugs, including new psychoactive substances (NPS), which mimic the effects of illegal drugs and pose a serious threat to human health.

LSD

LSD, which stands for lysergic acid diethylamide, is a potent hallucinogenic drug with a high potential for abuse. It is produced in secret labs and sold in various forms, including small decorative squares of blotter paper, stamps, tablets, sugar cubes, and liquid. LSD is also known by many street names, such as acid, dots, mellow yellow, blotter, cheer, lightning, similes, and tripper.

Taking LSD can cause a distorted perception of reality, with colours, sounds, objects, and time appearing strange and unsettling. The drug can also evoke a range of emotions, such as elation, wonder, vigour, empathy, anxiety, panic, and fear. The effects of LSD can last for several hours, and they can be unpredictable and severe, leading to good or bad trips depending on the user's experience.

LSD can be ingested by swallowing tablets or pellets or by adding drops of liquid to food or drink. It's a party drug.

LSD is usually smuggled into the country by air or at FPOs. The Chennai and Hyderabad police seized a sizable quantum of LSD decorative stamps.

Mephedrone

Mephedrone, also known as Meow Meow, is a powerful stimulant that is often compared to Cocaine and Ecstasy. It is a fine white, off-white, or yellowish powder that has a metallic taste and is commonly snorted or ingested by wrapping the powder in cigarette paper. Other names for Mephedrone include Bounce, Bubble, Charge Drone, M-Cat, M-Smack, MC, and White magic.

The drug produces intense euphoria, heightened sensitivity to touch, and sexual arousal, but also comes with risks such as anxiety, agitation, heart palpitations, dizziness, and sweating. Some users have reported blue or icy fingers and nosebleeds. Mephedrone has the potential to overstimulate the nervous system, leading to hallucinations, agitation, and convulsions.

> Production methods and high profits have made it popular among drug traffickers in India, as evidenced by a recent raid in which 225kg of mephedrone worth 1,125 crore was seized by the Gujarat anti-terrorist squad.

Methaqualone – Mandrax

Methaqualone, also known as Mandrax, is a sedative medication that was frequently prescribed in many countries before it was banned because of its highly addictive nature and propensity for abuse. The drug was previously very popular in the United States, Germany, and Japan and was one of the bestselling sedatives in these countries prior to its prohibition.

Mandrax has now become a renowned "party drug" and is frequently used in nightclubs across Europe, the United States, and South Africa because of the unique sense of euphoria it induces in users.

Presently, South Africa is the world's largest consumer of Mandrax, even though the drug is illegal in the country. In India, the production, possession, and transportation of Methaqualone are criminal offences under the NDPS Act. Nonetheless, it is believed the drug continues to be sold for exorbitant prices of a couple of thousands per gram and is abused at rave parties.

> Despite its prohibition, significant quantities of Methaqualone have been seized in India, with 3,000 kg from covert and clandestine factories in Vapi, Gujarat, in 2002, and 23,320 kg from a warehouse near Udaipur in 2016.

In 2019 more than 800 kg were seized in Pune. These seizures highlight the persistent demand for the drug.

ATS – Amphetamine-Type Stimulants

Ephedrine/Psuedo Ephedrine

Amphetamine

Methamphetamine

Ketamine

ATS—Amphetamine-Type Stimulants

It is a group of drugs that stimulate the central nervous system. The group includes drugs like Amphetamine, Methamphetamine, Phentermine, Methylphenidate, Dexamphetamine, and Ephedrine. It also includes Ecstasy-type substances like MDMA and MDA. The most commonly used substances in this group are Amphetamines, Methamphetamine, and Ecstasy.

> In 2020, a record amount of over 525 tons of ATS was seized globally.

The majority of ATS trafficking is dominated by Methamphetamine. From 2016 to 2020, authorities dismantled nearly 16,000 clandestine labs involved in ATS manufacturing across 45 countries. The sudden surge of abuse of these synthetic drugs has engulfed youngsters in India too. These drugs are highly addictive and cheaper in comparison to some other classes of drugs.

Methamphetamine

Methamphetamine production relies on various precursors, and the most commonly used precursors vary depending on the region. In Asia, Oceania, Africa, and most parts of Europe, Ephedrine and Pseudoephedrine are the primary precursors. India is one of the leading pharmaceutical manufacturing nations. As per the World Drug 2022 report recent data on seizures in 2020 suggest that pseudoephedrine preparations, mainly originating from India, are being used more frequently in the production of Methamphetamine.

> The drug mafias and drug traffickers from Myanmar-NE as well as Afghanistan-Iranian-Pakistani are actively involved in pushing "Meth" in the country.

There are frequent seizures across the nation which points to the growing menace of these synthetic drugs.

Moreover, since 2006, ketamine has been used in the form of pills containing a unique mixture of Cocaine called "CK1", especially in Goa. This mixture, also known as "Blizzard" and "Calvin Klein," is unique to the region.

Speed

Amphetamine sulphate, commonly known as "Speed", is a potent stimulant party drug, that is available as a powder or paste. Users report feeling alert and engaged in physical activities for extended periods of time. However, the drug can cause negative side effects such as psychosis, hallucinations, and depression.

Ecstasy

Ecstasy is a term that was initially used to refer to tablets that contain 3,4-Methylenedioxymethamphetamine, also known as MDMA. However, in recent years, a variety of different substances marketed as Ecstasy have emerged on the market. These products may contain MDMA or related substances such as MDA and MDEA, but the actual content is often unknown to the user. It is one of the most popular party drugs.

Spice

> Spice is a popular synthetic cannabinoid that mimics the effects of THC found in Marijuana but is much more potent and easier to overdose on.

It comes in solid and oil forms and is mixed with other ingredients, such as herbs or plant trimmings, to create a smoking mixture that looks similar to real herbal Cannabis. These smoking mixes are often sold in small, colourful sachets labelled as incense or herbal smoking combinations.

Synthetic cannabinoids are typically added to plant material by soaking or spraying, although in some cases the crystalline powder form may also be added. Recently, they have also been added to e-liquids and impregnated papers. Synthetic cannabinoids are primarily consumed through smoking, but oral use has also been reported.

Smoking blends containing synthetic cannabinoids are sold under various brand names such as Amsterdam Gold, K2, Spice, Tai High, and Hawaiian Haze, among others. These smoking blends can be consumed by smoking in a spliff, joint, pipe, or bong or vaping in an e-cigarette. **Some reports suggest that e-liquids containing synthetic cannabinoids have also been developed for use with standard e-cigarettes.**

Medicinal Prescription Drugs—Misuse and Abuse

The use of benzodiazepines, such as alprazolam and diazepam, is a common prescription for treating anxiety. However, it is found that these drugs are highly abused and as such are used without medical prescriptions.

> One of the most abused medicinal preparations is CBCS—codeine-based cough syrup.

Codeine is a pain reliever that can be taken in different forms such as tablets, syrup or liquid injections to treat moderate to severe pain. It is an opioid drug that is commonly used to alleviate physical discomfort, but unfortunately, it is also one of the most misused pharmaceuticals available. Some people use codeine as an antidepressant to cope with emotional distress, which poses a risk for addiction when using drugs to "numb out" negative emotions. It is one of the cheapest forms of drug as regards the cost and thus it is abused by many youngsters who look for a cheap source of drug abuse.

There has been a deep nexus between the drug mafias, drug distributors and stockists, certain chemist shops and many big pharma companies, which has been exposed from time to time by drug law enforcement agencies and police. Surprisingly, one hardly finds CBCS in any nearby chemist shop irrespective of the large-scale production by many pharma giants. However, year after year, thousands of bottles of illicit CBCS are being seized throughout the country. Recently in June 2022, 20,000 bottles of CBCS were seized at Murshidabad, Kolkata and 1,200 bottles of CBCS were seized in Bihar.

Yaba: The Crazy Drug Craze

In February 2021, the STF of the Kolkata police arrested five individuals and seized 1.5 lakh Yaba tablets with a market value of ₹7.50 crore from their possession. The BSF and Assam police seized vast quantities of synthetic narcotics in November 2021. They seized 26 packets containing 2,59,200 Yaba tablets worth ₹12.96 crore. Near the Indo-Bangladesh border in Tripura, the BSF seized 29,580 Yaba tablets worth ₹1.47 crore in December 2021. In Assam's Karim Ganj in January 2022, the BSF caught a drug dealer and recovered 26,000 Yaba tablets worth ₹1.30 crore from his possession. In May 2022, the BSF arrested an Indian woman with 5,620 Yaba tablets valued at ₹28 lakh near a petrol station in Bongaon, North 24-Parganas, West Bengal. The STF arrested four Murshidabad residents and recovered 30,000 yaba tablets from their possession in Siliguri. The Assam police claimed that a seizure of these drugs worth 160 crore was done in September 2022. The drug consignment was being smuggled across the borders from Myanmar to Mizoram.

So, what is this Yaba which has suddenly become the most sought-after drug?

Yaba, which literally translates to "crazy medication" is a cocktail of Methamphetamine and caffeine contained in tablet form.

Tablets of Yaba, which typically contain roughly 30 per cent Methamphetamine and caffeine, are often crushed and smoked, activating the central nervous system. Drug abusers notice a tremendous surge of energy, followed by increased activity, appetite reduction, and an overall feeling of well-being. After the effects of the drug have worn off, the drug addicts "crash" into extended periods of sleep and depression.

It is a very strong stimulant. Yaba is presently the most commonly misused type of Methamphetamine in Thailand, Laos, and Cambodia, as well as Vietnam and Myanmar, where it is primarily produced. However, Myanmar (Burma) is the epicentre of Yaba. India is also seeing a sudden surge in abuse of the new drug. The recent drug seizures are a testimony in itself.

> Myanmar (bordering India and Bangladesh), one of the world's largest producers of Methamphetamine, has no legitimate pharmaceutical industry, which means that domestic production of Methamphetamine in this area is totally dependent on the procurement of illegally diverted precursors and illicit active ingredients.

These are sourced from neighbouring countries. There are incidents reported where some of the pharma firms have illicitly diverted the precursors to these drug mafias.

NPS: New Psychoactive Substances

The illicit drug trade is becoming increasingly complex. Cannabis, Cocaine, and Heroin have been joined by hundreds of synthetic narcotics, the majority of which are not under international regulation. These are the new psychoactive drugs—NPS.

Each year, approximately 500 NPS are found on the international markets of member states. NPS has been reported in 111 countries and territories. Trends in the market for synthetic drugs evolve dramatically every year.

Synthetic drugs are one of the world's major drug concerns. In addition to synthetic cannabinoids, the ongoing expansion of the market for NPS in recent years has become a regulatory challenge and a major international concern. The expanding chemical diversity of NPS, as well as their unprecedented magnitude, complicates the tracking and analysis of this problem.

Every week, a new NPS is synthesized somewhere in the world.

The bulk of these NPS are not subject to international or national restrictions, posing a significant challenge to anti-drug agencies and regulatory authorities. In other words, because they have not been formally declared "illegal", they can simply escape and evade the regulations.

Designer Drugs

In the illicit market, NPS has been referred to as "designer drugs", "legal highs", "herbal highs", "bath salts", "research chemicals", and "laboratory reagents". To enhance a clear understanding of this issue, the UNODC only uses the term NPS, which is defined as "abuse substances, either pure or in a preparation, that are not controlled by the 1961 Single

Convention on Narcotic Drugs or the 1971 Convention on Psychotropic Substances but may pose a public health threat." The phrase "new" does not necessarily indicate to new innovations; numerous NPS were first synthesized 40 years ago; rather, it refers to compounds that have just entered the market and have not been listed under drug control conventions.

> Today there may be more than 1000 NPS and they constantly keep on evolving.

Here are a few examples of NPS sold globally:

a. **Synthetic cannabinoids**: These compounds generate effects comparable to THC, Cannabis's main psychoactive component. Synthetic cannabinoids are often laced into herbal products and marketed as spice, K2, Kronic, and so forth.

b. **Synthetic cathinone**: These are analogues/derivatives of the globally prohibited drug cathinone, which is one of the active ingredients in Khat. They have stimulant effects in general and include commonly reported NPS such as mephedrone.

c. **Ketamine**: Ketamine is a veterinary and human anaesthetic that functions as a stimulant in low dosages and a hallucinogen at large levels. It is one of the most common NPS in Asia.

d. **Phenethylamines**: This class of drugs includes Amphetamine and Methamphetamine-like compounds that have stimulant properties. However, modifying these chemicals may result in powerful hallucinogens.

e. **Piperazines**: Due to their stimulant characteristics, these compounds are commonly marketed as Ecstasy. This group's most regularly reported members are benzylpiperazine.

> India is one of the leading chemical and pharma manufacturers.

The pilferage of chemicals and pharma substances in the illicit market cannot be ruled out. In addition to making slight modifications to the molecules of recognized drugs, drug traffickers now utilize a vast amount of pharmaceutical and medical research to create new psychoactive substances. Despite the fact that the UNODC is working on an early detection system and that India, as a member state, is kept up to date on the latest advancements, NPS poses a substantial threat to India.

DRUG-RELATED PARAPHERNALIA

Vaping the E-cigarettes

The term "drug paraphernalia" refers to any equipment, accessory, product, or material that has been customized to prepare, administer, consume, smoke, inject, or hide prohibited drugs, psychotropics, or other narcotics. Metal, wood, acrylic, glass, stone, plastic, and ceramic pipes, roach clips, small spoons, bongs, cigarette papers, and electronic cigarettes are typical types of drug paraphernalia. In addition to online sellers, cigarette shops, *paan* shops, and gift and novelty shops sell paraphernalia. One may use aluminium foil to smoke Heroin or inhale Methamphetamine vapours. Rolling papers are used to roll and smoke Cannabis joints. Hookahs and pipes are used to smoke Marijuana, Cocaine, and other illegal narcotics. A syringe is used to inject substances such as Heroin straight into the body.

However, the most popular are e-cigarettes—electronic cigarettes, or vapes—battery-powered devices used to smoke illegal drugs or banned psychotropic substances of abuse.

In July 2022, Hyderabad Airport Customs officials intercepted five travellers attempting to smuggle e-cigarettes worth ₹25 lakh.

> The DRI seized electronic cigarettes worth ₹48 crore at the Mundra Port in Gujarat in September 2022. More than two lakh e-cigarettes of different Chinese brands were seized.

Earlier in September 2022, DRI investigators intercepted a trailer on the way from Ahmedabad to Mumbai near Surat and recovered 85,600 e-cigarettes worth ₹20 crore. In a follow-up search near Mumbai, they recovered two crore worth of electronic cigarettes from Bhiwandi. According to reports, these goods were also smuggled into the country via the port of Mundra.

In the same month, DRI agents at Kempe Gowda International Airport intercepted a passenger travelling from Dubai to Bengaluru with 840 e-cigarettes, often referred to as vapes, valued at over ₹16 lakh (KIA).

One may have many questions in this regard:

What exactly are these e-cigarettes?

Why is there a sudden demand for these?

Who is trying to push it and smuggle it into the Indian market?

What is the legal aspect of e-cigarettes?

Electronic cigarettes (or "vape pens") convert a liquid into a vapour that is inhaled. The liquid (called e-liquid or vape juice) may include nicotine, Marijuana distillate, Hashish oil, or any such drug.

Typically, Marijuana is rolled and smoked like cigarettes (joints or unfiltered cigarettes) or placed in cigars, pipes (bowls), or pipes (bongs). Utilizing a vaporizer to consume Marijuana or harsher Marijuana extracts has grown in popularity recently called "vaping" or "dabbing". Inhaling the vapour that is produced by an electronic cigarette is referred to as vaping. It's quite frequent among young people.

> Dangerously potent synthetic Marijuana consists of man-made substances that are chemically related to THC.

These substances are referred to as K2, Spice, and Herbal incense. They may be so strong that fatal overdoses have occurred.

E-cigarettes were initially marketed as a tool to wean people off of smoking, however, studies reveal that many individuals are hooked to them rather than utilizing them as a weaning technique.

The best way to prevent youngsters and nonsmokers from taking up vaping and developing a drug habit that would increase their risk of converting to harmful smoking is to ban e-cigarettes nationwide.

> On September 18, 2019, the Government of India issued an ordinance to ban e-cigarettes—The Prohibition of Electronic Cigarettes (Production, Manufacture, Import, Export, Transport, Sale, Distribution, Storage and Advertisement) Act, 2019 came into force.

This is where Newton's Law came into play, "every action has an equal and opposite response," resulting in a massive grey and illicit market. The smugglers began to see a massive profit opportunity. Various methods are used in pushing and smuggling e-cigarettes in order to avoid detection by customs officials. Recent massive seizures demonstrate that all feasible ports, methods, and means are being exploited to push it into the grey market. It also demonstrates that there is a rise in demand in the market.

> E-cigarette addiction among school students appears to be on the rise, which is a disturbing trend.

Before the COVID-19 pandemic, it would have been one in 1,000 students, but sources say the figures may be ranging from 60 to more now. High school students have been spotted carrying e-cigarettes to campuses to flaunt them, which is quite alarming given how far this drug epidemic has spread.

Section 4

In the Shadows of Darknet

DEEP WEB

The COVID-19 pandemic in 2020 and subsequent lockdowns in many countries have caused a decline in conventional drug trafficking methods, leading to changes in drug prices. Nonetheless, the current technological era has given rise to an increase in cybercrime, particularly in the form of darknet retail sales.

Purchases and sales of drugs and NPS over the Internet involve both the open net (using encrypted communications) and the darknet, which forms part of the deep web. The deep web, invisible web, or hidden web are parts of the World Wide Web whose contents are not indexed by standard web search engines. This is in contrast to the "surface web", which is accessible to anyone using the Internet. It is estimated that the surface web is only the tip of the iceberg, accounting for less than 15 per cent of all content and information on the internet. The deep web's content is hidden behind HTTP forms and includes uses such as webmail, online banking, private or otherwise restricted access social-media pages and profiles, some web forums that require registration to view content and services that users must pay for and are protected by paywalls, such as video on demand and some online magazines and newspapers. Most government data are also a part of the deep web.

The Onion Router (Tor)

The main characteristic and comparative advantage of darknet markets is their perceived anonymity. Darknet trafficking also overcomes the challenge of sellers and buyers having to be in the same place at the same time. Drug abusers and drug peddlers, seeking to purchase narcotics on the darknet generally do so using The Onion Router (Tor) to disguise their identity. Tor is free and open-source software that allows for anonymous communication. Like peeling an onion layer by layer until you find nothing at the end of it, Tor does precisely what its name implies. It routes Internet traffic over a free, global, volunteer overlay network of over 6,000 relays to mask a user's location and use it as a tool for network surveillance or traffic analysis. Tor makes it more difficult to track the user's Internet activities. Tor's intended usage is to safeguard its users' privacy, freedom, and capacity to conduct secret communication by leaving their Internet activity unmonitored.

Darknet Markets

Cryptocurrencies may then be used to purchase other goods and services or swap for various national currencies. Darknet platforms connect anonymous suppliers with anonymous customers. Although some darknet drug sales are from dealer to dealer, it appears that the vast majority are still from dealer to user. Drug trafficking has been characterized by a high turnover of drugs over the darknet. Darknet markets continue to vanish as a result of law enforcement, exit scams, and voluntary closures, while new ones emerge. A previous analysis of 103 darknet markets selling drugs over the period 2010-2017 revealed that those markets were, on average, active for just over eight months, and their average lifespan does not appear to have increased in recent years and most of the previously important dark-net markets have disappeared.

Some of the largest darknet markets for drug listings were Silk Route, Alpha Bay, Nucleus, Dream Market, Crypto Market, Hansa, Python, French Darknet, Darknet Heroes League, Trade Route, Valhalla, and Berlusconi Market.

Silk Road was a prominent digital black-market website for hosting money laundering and illicit drug transactions utilizing Bitcoin. Silk Road, widely recognized as the first darknet market, debuted in 2011 and was finally taken down by the FBI in 2013. Ross William Ulbricht, who is now serving a life term in jail for his part in Silk Road, established it. Several additional darknet marketplaces have sprouted since then.

Empire Market is still small compared with Alpha Bay and Dream Market, but it appears to have been growing over the past few months. As changes in darknet markets take place extremely quickly, it remains to be seen whether the platform, which was founded a few years ago, will emerge as the dominant darknet market in the near future, like Silk Road, Alpha Bay, and Dream Market, before it disappears into oblivion within a few months, like many other platforms that were hyped for short periods.

For years, the darknet has been used to buy and sell narcotics without the involvement of many of the regular players.

They carry narcotics to anonymous post office boxes, where end users pick them up, using private or public postal services. Parallel Bitcoin transactions on the darknet are used to make the payment in real-time.

Half of Internet users continue to use the same type of drugs they used prior to obtaining drugs through the darknet. More than a quarter of those who started using drugs now report that they consume a wider range of drugs. The darknet may be developing into an alternative source of drugs, such as friends, acquaintances, or street drug dealers, for people who have not previously used drugs.

Law enforcement actions or exit scams have forced the closure of many large darknet marketplaces since mid-2017. This has resulted in a short-term decrease in darknet drug trafficking.

In 2020, however, the number of people purchasing drugs on the darknet has risen.

While COVID-19-related limitations were in place, trafficking operations on the darknet increased, especially purchases by end-users who find it difficult to contact street sellers. Retail sales of Cannabis were a major factor in this. As a consequence of the lockdown limitations, sales of Marijuana on the dark web seem to be up. Activity on three darknet drug marketplaces in Europe seems to have surged in the first quarter of 2020. It is obvious that retail purchases of Cannabis have risen. According to an analysis of email addresses found on eight major websites, China accounts for 9.14 per cent of the global darknet drug market. The United

States and Europe account for the largest share 34 per cent, followed by the Netherlands and the UK with 32 per cent. India has also seen an increase in darknet users in the past few years.

While established criminal organizations and networks are involved in poly-drug trafficking, the rise of darknet marketplaces may have also facilitated the selling of drugs. Most sellers on these platforms have a wide selection of drugs available for purchase. Poly-drug sales are common on the darknet, as is the case with other illicit drug markets.

Darknet Drug Syndicate in India

Recently, the NCB busted a major drug trafficking network on the darknet after a four-month investigation, arresting 22 active members of the syndicate from various states, some of whom had ties to source countries such as the United States, United Kingdom, the Netherlands, and Poland.

Suspects were detained after raids took place in several places at the same time in Gujarat, Maharashtra, and Karnataka, as well as Delhi-NCR and Punjab, Jharkhand, West Bengal, Rajasthan, and Uttar Pradesh. This shows how the whole country is in this deep menace of drugs. The majority of those arrested are highly qualified professionals which is more worrisome. The accused range in age from 22 to 35 years old and work as engineers, doctors, financial advisors, artists, and musicians.

Commercial quantities of LSD, MDMA, Ganja, Charas, Cannabis Paste, Alprazolam, Hashish, Ganja Chocolates, and Cocaine were seized along with cash and cryptocurrency worth crore.

The modus operandi is simple. The drug smugglers deliver the contraband to their customers' homes because of the many vulnerabilities in the courier and postal systems. Many times, parents or other family members of the individuals engaged were completely unaware of what was taking place.

> Names of well-known courier firms were being abused to send narcotics in nicely packed boxes containing things like toys and stationery or everyday necessities.

> Earlier a sophisticated drug trafficking network was discovered in Ahmedabad, which made use of modern technologies such as cryptocurrency payments and the darknet to deliver illegal drugs via air freight couriers.

The masterminds behind the operation were highly educated individuals from affluent families, and the investigation uncovered the sale of different types of drugs, including hybrid Ganja, American Charas, Malana Charas, and Psychotropic Magic Mushrooms, to college students from various institutions in Ahmedabad and Gandhinagar. The total worth of the smuggled drugs was estimated to be more than ₹100 crore.

Darkathon

The NCB initiated a 'Darkathon' for cyber specialists to create effective methods to unravel the anonymity of markets on the dark web days after uncovering a drug ring operating on the darknet. The effort aims to engage students, youngsters, and technical specialists to develop efficient solutions for decrypting darknet markets' anonymity. Their "solution" must crawl the dark web and find darknet markets where drugs are sold, as well as drug traffickers in India and the drugs they are selling, and the digital footprints of active drug traffickers, so they can keep track of them. There is attractive prize money for participants.

Time for a strong cyber-wing

The NCB has been given the go-ahead to increase its staff by 1,800 and set up a cyber-wing, where experts will track and crack down on drug smuggling done through the darknet and cryptocurrencies. The NCB is planning to establish a cyber wing that will be directed by a dedicated deputy D-G level officer and will focus only on drug-related crimes that are facilitated by the Internet, particularly on the darknet. The wing will work closely with intelligence agencies and will consist of about a dozen officers. The wing will detect and investigate drug trafficking cases involving cryptocurrencies and the darknet effectively. Apart from a specific lab to deal with the online drug trade, the cyber wing will have cyber-forensic capabilities such as retrieval of erased data from laptops, mobile phones, and servers, various decryption tools, and cyber-training sessions.

Cryptocurrency—An Innovative Drug Currency

A cryptocurrency is a digital or virtual currency that is protected by encryption, making counterfeiting or double-spending practically impossible. Many cryptocurrencies are decentralized networks built on blockchain technology, which is a distributed ledger enforced by a network of computers. Cryptocurrencies are distinguished by the fact that they are typically not issued by any central authority, making them potentially impervious to government meddling or manipulation. Cryptocurrencies have a number of advantages, including cheaper and quicker money transactions and decentralized systems that do not have a single point of failure and maintain anonymity at the same time. The most valued cryptocurrency is Bitcoin. It was created in 2008 by an unknown individual named Satoshi Nakamoto and published in a white paper. Today's market has hundreds of cryptocurrencies. But there is a flip side too.

Crypto Protocols

Cryptocurrency is the new drug money—an innovative drug currency that has deeply penetrated the Indian sub-continent.

In April 2022, the Indian Parliament was informed that the NCB and CBIC discovered a ₹2.2 crore cryptocurrency payment in 11 drug trafficking cases.

The Minister of State for Finance stated in a written reply to the Lok Sabha that the government is taking efforts to curb such usage by providing training for field officers on cyber and forensic technology, as well as electronic evidence collecting.

In 2021 too concerns have been expressed by the Parliamentary Committee on Home Affairs about the growing use of digital currency and darknet for drug trafficking. In a report submitted to the Parliament, the committee expresses concern about the increasing use of cryptocurrencies and the darknet for drug trafficking. Further, technology is being leveraged by drug traffickers to maintain anonymity, making it difficult to track the movement of drugs.

There was a buzz that the government may come out with a Cryptocurrency and Regulation of the Official Digital Currency Bill as it seeks to create a framework for the creation of the official digital currency to be issued by RBI. There are also discussions to prohibit private cryptocurrencies but allow exceptions to promote the underlying technology of cryptocurrency and its uses. Regulation and protocol are the need of the hour.

Recently, in March 2023, cryptocurrency has been brought under the ambit of the anti-money laundering laws of PMLA.

Crypto-Cannabis

> In India, where the government has imposed strict regulations on cryptocurrencies, the West has opened it up for buying and selling Marijuana.

The West has seen an unprecedented increase in the use of cryptocurrency in both the licit and illicit drug trades. Although Marijuana is legal in many states, the federal government of the United States has not decriminalized the substance.

Because banks cannot lawfully undertake Marijuana-related business, Marijuana-based operators and consumers can utilize Marijuana-specific cryptocurrency for their transactions.

> PotCoin, CannabisCoin, DopeCoin, HempCoin, and CannaCoin are some of the most popular Marijuana-based cryptocurrencies.

PotCoin was one of the first Marijuana-themed cryptocurrencies, launched in January 2014. It was created to help consumers who wanted to buy legal Marijuana. PotCoin is traded directly between users, without a bank or clearinghouse. It now trades on three exchanges and uses proof-of-stake, allowing holders to mine or validate blocks based on their holdings. PotCoin claims transaction times of 40 seconds, which is fast compared to Bitcoin's. To improve the user experience, the cryptocurrency introduced HD wallets, quicker network synchronization, and reduced synch times in early 2019. It launched a new platform on the

Nexus Network for its desktop and mobile wallets on April 20, 2021. DopeCoin users can transact pseudo-anonymously in under a minute. HempCoin is another popular crypto used for buying and selling Marijuana.

Uncovering the World of Drug Smuggling

Modus Operandi—The Art of Concealment

A team of officials from the Delhi Police's Special Cell arrived at the Jawaharlal Nehru Port in Mumbai on September 16, 2022. To the astonishment of customs officials, they were there to inspect a shipment of 20,000 kg of liquorice roots, commonly known as *jyeshtahmadh* (*mulethi*). The shipments had already been routinely inspected by the port's customs officers, and nothing improper was found. The police officers examined the container from every possible angle, including the body cavities, if any. Finally, they started to examine every *mulethi* stick in the shipment, which weighed around 20,000 kg in total. They observed that the colour of certain liquorice root sticks was darker than that of others. The team was finally able to detect Heroin in all of the darker-coloured liquorice sticks after a laborious, all-night-long exercise and unrelenting effort.

The liquorice sticks were soaked in Heroin. Heroin with an estimated quantity of 345 kg worth over ₹1,725 crore in the international market was recovered.

This was a unique modus operandi, where the *mulethi* was soaked in Heroin and then sundried. Had the consignments been cleared undetected, the drug traffickers would have successfully recovered the heroin through various extraction methods.

A modus operandi (often shortened to MO), is the mode of operation usually the criminal adopts to evade detection by the agencies. In drug trafficking, it's the fine art of concealment of drugs.

Drug traffickers are using novel MO to conceal drugs. In September 2021, the Iranian-Afghani drug cartel camouflaged almost three metric tons of heroin with talc consignment which was ultimately seized at the Mundra Port. The DRI seized 395 kg of Heroin-laced thread at Gujarat's Pipavav Port.

The following are some of the various MOs followed by drug cartels to smuggle their drugs.

Soaked

In July 2019, the Delhi police team conducted a thorough search at the customs bonded area in Panvel, Mumbai. A cargo that was imported from the Bandar Abbas port of Iran contained some 260 jute bags carrying basil seeds. The 260 jute bags were found to be soaked in 130 kilos of Afghan Heroin.

The Irani-Afghan drug cartel seems to have acquired this technique of soaking from the Colombian and Mexican drug cartels. In several nations, drug-soaked clothing, sweaters, and T-shirts have been reported. A British man of Pakistani origin was recently nabbed for attempting to smuggle 24 kg of Heroin out of Pakistan soaked in 25 jackets. In May 2022 a courier was arrested trying to smuggle 55 pounds of Heroin-soaked apparel into Houston.

Recently, 395 kg of Heroin-soaked in yarns/threads was seized in Gujarat port.

Cavities

Another modus operandi adopted by drug traffickers is concealing in specially made cavities. In July 2021, officials uncovered the drugs concealed in specifically made cavities of luxury sedans such as the Toyota Camry, Honda Civic, Toyota Alti, and Toyota Corolla.

> Customs officers seized 300 kg of Ganja secreted in a specialized cavity in a truck in Barrackpore, West Bengal in March 2022.

In April 2022, the NCB caught a Heroin trafficker near Dimapur. The narcotics were hidden in a secret compartment of his car. In May 2022, the NCB apprehended a drug trafficker with 28 kg of pure Opium near the Assam border while attempting to smuggle the Opium in a carefully designed covert cavity in his SUV automobile. In the same month, two traffickers were apprehended near Salem, Tamil Nadu, with Heroin hidden in a secret compartment in their vehicle.

> Recently, in March 2023, 20 crore worth of drugs were seized from a black Scorpio, concealed in the cavities and tyre stepney. In the same month, 100 kilos of pure opium, worth 20 crore were seized from a vehicle having secret cavities.

Drug traffickers who travel by air frequently hide drugs in false luggage bottoms. In September 2022, a passenger who flew down from Dubai to Bengaluru carrying 840 e-cigarettes, also known as vapes, hidden in the false bottom of his baggage was caught. In an operation code-named 'Black & White,' the DRI confiscated 55 kg of Heroin from an imported cargo consignment that was declared to include trolley bags.

> The drugs were secreted inside the hollow metal tubes of 126 trolley bags, making detection extremely difficult.

Two African nationals were caught at the Rajiv Gandhi International Airport in Hyderabad with ₹80 crore worth of Cocaine. The false bottoms of their trolleys were stuffed with four kilos of pure Cocaine. Heroin was discovered in the false bottom of a passenger's bag at the Mumbai International Airport in April 2022, revealing a similar technique of operation by the drug traffickers. Two Kenyan travellers were apprehended at Ahmedabad airport with 8.5 kg of Heroin secreted in a false compartment of their luggage.

Swallowers—Body Packers

> Drug traffickers of African descent employ one of the riskiest methods of operation. They are referred to as "swallowers" or "body packers".

They ingest the drugs and transport them into their bodies. Before boarding a flight, they typically consume drugs packaged in condoms and in the shape of large-size capsules with some edible lubricants. Throughout the duration of the flight, they will not eat or drink anything to prevent the urge to defecate. Once they reach their destination, they will excrete these drug-filled capsules. If the drug capsule inadvertently breaks or ruptures inside the body, the outcome could be fatal.

In April 2022, a Tanzanian national was intercepted by the NCB officers. About 1.34 kg of cocaine, having an international value of more than ₹10 crore were recovered from him. He had swallowed drug-filled capsules.

Air Customs Officers intercepted a passenger from Sharjah on May 17, 2022. The passenger swallowed 63 capsules containing 794.64 grams of Heroin worth ₹5.56 crore, which was recovered/seized. Customs officers of the Air Intelligence Unit (AIU) at Coimbatore Airport intercepted a Ugandan woman who landed in Coimbatore on May 6, 2022. The passenger had swallowed 81 Methamphetamine capsules. Upon purging, 892 grams of Methamphetamine worth ₹2.68 crore was recovered and confiscated.

Drug traffickers continuously employ innovative and unconventional methods to hide their drug shipments from law enforcement agencies. This poses a significant challenge to the officers who must remain vigilant to uncover and disrupt their schemes. Authorities must stay ahead of drug traffickers by using effective intelligence gathering and advanced technologies to keep the nation safe from this ever-growing drug menace.

Narco-Terrorism—The K2 Factor

September 2022 saw one of the nation's largest seizures of Methamphetamine, a potent psychoactive substance. Delhi Police's Special Cell recovered 310 kg of the drug valued at a whopping ₹1,200 crore after intercepting two Afghan nationals linked to a multinational narco-terror network. Due to the drug's striking resemblance to silica, the contraband was concealed in bags displaying silica marks. While the drug cartel base was in Iran, the proceeds from sales were channelled via hawala networks to Turkey, Portugal, Pakistan, Afghanistan, and Iran.

In a subsequent operation, 1.7 kg of Heroin-coated dried fruits were recovered from the boot of a white Toyota Etios parked in Greater Noida.

Exactly a year back, the DRI made India's largest drug haul to date in September 2021: 3,000 kilos of Heroin, estimated at over ₹21,000 crore in the international market, was smuggled into the country through Iran in a shipment of semi-processed talc stones.

> The NIA conducted pan-India searches. The NIA uncovered that drug money from India was repatriated to Afghanistan to support terror operations.

The drug traffickers cleverly forged dozen of documents, including GST invoices, custom clearance certificates, and company records, greased many palms, and rented premises in Delhi to store the drugs before distributing them in the Indian market through a network of peddlers. The alleged drug cartel was as large as it was intricate, with links ranging from Afghanistan, Iran, and Pakistan to Punjab, Uttar Pradesh, and Tamil Nadu. International drug traffickers from Afghanistan and Iran smuggle large amounts of Heroin into India to make profit, which is subsequently moved to other nations. These traffickers established links with terrorist groups in Pakistan and received active backing from them to carry out subversive actions against India. When additional information began to arrive, the situation became murkier. It was discovered that a similar cargo was imported into the same port a few months earlier, which went undetected by the customs officers stationed at Mundra Port. The investigations revealed that a similar drug consignment was clandestinely smuggled at Kolkata port too. Two huge drug consignments slipped through the customs checks and entered the market.

> Narco-terrorism is the link between drugs and terrorism. Terrorism requires large quantities of money to operate.

Because obtaining that quantity from official and legal sources is difficult, terrorists seek support from drug syndicates and underworld dons.

The narcotics revenues are being utilized to destabilize India by the enemy countries. It brings in large sums of money, and that too in hard cash. Narcotic drugs are the most profitable commodity, generating instant money with hardly any paperwork. The commercial transaction is completed in cash, and no documentation is left as proof in the event of legal action. Drug revenues are laundered via a plethora of legitimate and criminal financial institutions and nefarious firms.

> Narco-terrorism tactics have currently undergone a paradigm shift.

Pakistan is using narco-terrorism as a proxy against India. We all know how the drug menace has plagued the youth of Punjab. Heroin consumption has unfortunately increased by 2,000 per cent in the Kashmir Valley during the last five years. There has been a startling rise in narcotics abuse across people of all socio-economic strata in the Valley. There is always a new drug addict checking into the drug rehab centre in Kashmir every single hour. While the Oral Substitution Therapy Centre at Srinagar's Government Medical College saw just 489 patients in 2016, that number surpassed 10,000 by 2021. The security forces and the administration of Jammu and Kashmir have been shaken by this worrisome increase only in the previous five years.

Pakistan has recently utilized a twin tactic of delivering both narcotics and guns to keep the war alive and to rip the valley's social fabric apart. The most often used narcotic in Kashmir is Heroin trafficked from Pakistan. Cross-border drug smuggling offers financial fuel to terrorism and, if not nipped in the bud, has the potential to jeopardize the lives of the region's children. Heroin-related drug profits fuel separatist actions and propagate other centrifugal tendencies. In June 2021, a narco-terror module was discovered in the

Baramulla area, resulting in the arrest of 10 individuals in possession of ₹45 crore worth of Heroin, as well as four pistols and Chinese grenades. This terror cell was active across the whole of Jammu & Kashmir and beyond the union territory. Pakistan-based terrorist organizations and their supporters are trafficking narcotics into volatile Jammu and Kashmir to finance their operations after Indian agents cut down most of their funding avenues, including the frequently used hawala method.

> The epicentre of this narco-trade is the Shopian area of southern Kashmir, also known as the apple bowl, around 50 km from Srinagar.

Shopian is a desirable area for drug traffickers since it is a reasonably prosperous, area that trades the renowned Kashmiri apple from its extensive plantations. An intelligence assessment revealed that narcotics are supplied cheaply in quantity to entice peddlers, allowing them to profit more than those who deliver the material, who are mostly Pakistani militants in south Kashmir. Almost typically, the initial dosage is provided at no cost. Once someone becomes addicted, he begins purchasing. Thus, the cycle begins, and narcotics become a primary source of funding for terrorists.

> After brainwashing and indoctrinating the fragile minds of Jammu and Kashmir's youngsters, Pakistan now seeks to poison their blood. The first K stands for Kashmir.

Pakistan's hostility against India facilitates the concurrent expansion of drug trafficking and terrorist operations in the area. India's two border states, Kashmir and Punjab, were almost always targeted by terrorism and narcotics smuggling. Despite the fact that Punjab has not suffered an increase in terrorist activity in recent years, there is not much doubt that the Khalistan movement frequently erupts in the state. The relationship between Khalistan organisations, ISI, and traffickers is yielding easy drug money to fund militancy in Punjab while ruining the young via drug addiction.

> In recent years, drug use in border regions, particularly Punjab, has exploded.

The frequency and volume of drug seizures, however, have recently risen. Terrorists in Punjab formed an "unholy alliance" with drug dealers during the peak of the Khalistan uprising. The narcotics trade was utilized to get weaponry from Pakistan. Many of the traffickers apprehended by the authorities admitted that they had been granted entry over the border by the opposing authorities in exchange for promises to provide weapons to terrorist groups in India. Drug traffickers are still being used to smuggle weapons and money to terrorist groups, despite the fact that the security forces in Punjab have apprehended the militants there. Unfortunately, Punjab is witnessing a rise in the Khalistan movement once again. Recent years have seen a surge in drugs and arms dropping from across borders using high-tech drones.

Drones—A New High-Tech Gadget in the Hands of Narco-Terrorists

The NIA conducted raids in Punjab and found evidence of gangsters turned terrorists in Pakistan using China-made drones to smuggle arms, ammunition, and drugs across the border into Punjab. These drones are challenging to detect due to their small size, low sound, and ability to fly sub-radar. The BSF and Punjab police's intelligence wing noticed hundreds of such drone activities along the border. Most cross-border consignments by ISI and Pakistan-based militant groups are delivered through drones.

> The drones are being actively used across the borders in Rajasthan, Punjab, Jammu, and Kashmir for drug smuggling.

The analysis of the recovered drone revealed that it had a payload drop system attached to it, which could drop the payload upon receiving a signal. For example, a drone, manufactured by Da-Jiang Innovations in Shenzhen, China, could take off with a 9 kg weight and had a maximum flight time of 31 minutes, with a maximum speed of 82.8 km/ hour. These drones have a holding and releasing mechanism, which is remotely controlled. The Pakistani drug traffickers use these high-tech drones and drop the drugs at pinpointed pre-decided location and their associates and drug traffickers from the Indian side of the border, are informed of the GPS locations. Drug smugglers are now using such high-tech drones for drug smuggling.

Recently, in March 2023, BSF caught 10 kilos of Heroin worth more than 45 crore, in the international market, in three separate incidents of a drone dropping within 24 hours. A drone carrying two packets of Heroin weighing 1.6 kg, which was recovered by the BSF, was sent for examination to a forensics workshop in New Delhi.

> The finding baffled all the agencies. According to its logs, the drone had made 36 flights, indicating that the said drone was used for drug smuggling almost 36 times and drugs worth crores of rupees were smuggled across the Pakistan-India borders before it could be caught.

It is reported that hundreds of such drones have been sighted in the past few years.

According to reports in July 2019, Pakistan-based Khalistani militants are importing narcotics into India to fund terror operations in Punjab. Three incidents were attributed to Khalistan Commando Force, a terrorist organization located in Lahore since 1994. Six Pakistani fishermen were caught in May 2019 on the Gujarat border for smuggling 218 kg of drugs. On May 26, Maldivian authorities apprehended an Iranian boat carrying a Pakistani citizen and recovered a big quantum of narcotics destined for India. Based on information provided by Indian intelligence, the Sri Lankan coast guard captured 50 kg of Heroin from a Pakistani boat on July 10th. According to sources, the commander of the

Khalistan Liberation Force was assassinated in Pakistan due to a feud between two groups over control of drug money.

> The Ministry of Home Affairs (MHA) identified nine individuals linked with the Khalistani movement as terrorists in July 2020. Two of the nine people were labelled as terrorists because of their participation in narcotics trafficking and anti-India activities.

The second K stands for Khalistani terrorists. The Delhi Police, the NIA, and other federal agencies have shown how the Pakistani government and its intelligence agency, ISI, were engaged in the scheme to disrupt peace in Punjab. According to the reports the Pakistani government has been colluding for the previous six years and misled Punjab's young.

> The Pakistani government and the ISI established a K-2 (Kashmir-Khalistan) desk to destabilize Punjab and Kashmir.

In a recent turn of events, the Jammu and Kashmir Police unearthed a diabolical narco-terror module in Poonch, situated in proximity to the Line of Control (LoC). The operation yielded an impressive haul of 7 kg of Heroin, a hefty sum of nearly ₹2 crore, and an arsenal of weapons and ammunition, shedding light on a rather sinister and disturbing trend wherein drugs and weapons are being smuggled concurrently from Pakistan. While the weapons are being disseminated to the terrorists, the revenue accrued from the drug trade is remitted to the handlers across the border, with the remainder being disbursed among the peddlers.

Investigations have uncovered the intricate web of interstate connections involved in drug trafficking, particularly linked to Punjab. The NIA too found the nexus between the Afghani drug cartel, Pakistan, and drug mafias in Punjab, during the 3000 kg heroin investigation. Narcotics are almost conjoined with terrorists.

The finances generated from this pernicious enterprise are being channelled to sustain terrorism in Jammu and Kashmir, with Pakistani handlers siphoning off a considerable chunk of the profits to back terrorist groups operating from across the border. Such brazen activities necessitate prompt and coordinated action from various agencies to plug the inflow of illicit drugs and arms into the country and to curtail the funding of terrorism in the region.

OUR NEIGHBORS—DOUBLE TROUBLE

All nations desire that their neighbours thrive and live in peace. But when there is trouble—political instability, economic turbulence, a decline in morals, military interference, poverty, crime, and unrest—in the neighbouring countries, it makes things difficult. India is sandwiched between such countries. On the one side, it is surrounded by the Golden Crescent, a major hub for illicit Opium poppy cultivation in the world. This area spans the mountainous borders of Afghanistan and Pakistan and extends into eastern Iran, making it a key connecting point for Central, South, and Western Asia.

The Golden Triangle is on the opposite side. It is surrounded by Thailand, Laos, and Myanmar. Myanmar's Shan State is said to be the world's largest producer of Methamphetamine. Not only are these countries in serious economic and political instability, but they are also the world's largest producers of illicit drugs and narcotics.

Afghanistan, Pakistan, and Myanmar have all been actively involved in drug smuggling into India.

Opiate trafficking (Opium, Morphine, and Heroin) is possibly Afghanistan's most lucrative criminal economic sector. The estimated yield of Opium in 2021 was 6,800 tons.

This quantity of Opium may be transformed into around 600 to 700 tons of pure Heroin. The international street price for one kilogram of Heroin is believed to be between five and seven crore of rupees. According to these calculations, one can envision the financial gains. In recent years, the rise of Methamphetamine synthesis in Afghanistan has added another layer of complexity to the country's illegal drug industry and raised the danger to nations in the area and beyond. In Afghanistan, the production of Methamphetamine has increased dramatically in recent years, as shown by seizures both within and outside the nation.

Afghanistan provides more than 85 per cent of the world's Opium output, supplying Heroin to vast consumer markets in neighbouring nations. All actions associated with drug supply chains provide financial advantages for individuals concerned, from cultivation and manufacture through local distribution and worldwide drug trafficking. Without question, narcotics trafficking is a major contributor to Afghanistan's economy. In recent years, the Iran-Afghanistan drug cartel has been very active in trafficking large quantities of narcotics into our country.

Myanmar borders the northeastern Indian states of Nagaland, Mizoram, Manipur, and Arunachal Pradesh. This roughly 1,643-kilometer-long Indo-Myanmar border is believed to be the transit point for drug smuggling into the country's northeast. Several kilometres of the Indo-Myanmar border remain unfenced, allowing international drug traffickers operating in Myanmar to smuggle illicit substances into India.

It is believed that Delhi, Mumbai, and Kolkata drug cartels have allegedly invested large sums in the Golden Triangle.

It appears that the intelligence services warned of a "new connection" between north-eastern insurgency groups and drug peddlers who had shifted shipping routes. Drug trafficking is one of the insurgency organizations' main financing sources. Moreh is a border town situated on the border between India and Myanmar. Moreh is a significant trade hub between India and Myanmar. Tamu, also known as Tat Mu, is a town in northwestern Burma, close to the border with the eastern Indian state of Manipur. This route is used to illegally smuggle narcotics such as Heroin and Amphetamine-type drugs across borders. According to reports, there are many illicit crossover points between Moreh and Tamu. These border crossings are mostly exploited for smuggling. As a result, a large number of narcotics reach Imphal, which then leads to Kohima and Dimapur, where they are transported by railways to Assam. From there, the drugs are distributed across the rest of India.

Burma (Myanmar) is the largest producer of Methamphetamine in the world.

Yaba is a cocktail of Methamphetamine and caffeine contained in tablet form. It is the largest producer of the illicit drug Yaba. In a combined operation, the BSF and Customs department confiscated 17,000 Yaba pills manufactured in Myanmar from a residence in the Tripura district of

Sepahijala. Earlier, in the same area, the BSF recovered 28,000 Yaba pills worth ₹1.40 crore.

Yaba is in great demand in Bangladesh as well. Youths in Bangladesh see Yaba-Ecstasy use as a trend indicative of affluence. Myanmar's drug traffickers use Rohingya refugees to carry Yaba from Myanmar into Bangladesh. Investigations have revealed that the Yaba is trafficked into India through Bangladesh. In February 2021, the Kolkata Police STF arrested five individuals and seized around 1,50,000 Yaba tablets with a market value of ₹7.50 crore from their possession.

Economic measures are also crucial in the context of India's and Myanmar's potential susceptibilities. Priority should be given to identifying the drug manufacturing and supply chain, as well as better engaging young people participating in illegal activities.

Additionally, Nepal is a traditional supplier of Cannabis, including both the Weed (Marijuana) and resin variants of the plant (Hashish). Its porous border with India is being abused by narcotics cartels on both sides.

On top of that, we have Pakistan as a neighbour, which is unquestionably at the forefront and the primary cause of narco-terrorism we encounter in our nation, India.

> Indisputable evidence suggests that India's neighbours have contributed significantly to the current era's drug issue.

THE FOREIGN HAND: NIGERIANS—REVERSE SMUGGLING

The NCB informed their counterpart, a senior drug enforcement official in Nigeria about more than 8,000 Nigerians who had overstayed their Indian visas by at least two years and were involved in drug-related and financial crimes. This revelation underscores the increasing concern about international drug trafficking. This revelation highlights the need for greater collaboration and coordination between countries to effectively combat the drug menace and ensure public safety. This highlights the pressing need for international cooperation and collaboration to tackle the issue of drug trafficking and guarantee public safety and it serves as a wake-up call for the urgent need for a united front against the drug threat.

Indian authorities also discussed with their Nigerian counterparts the problem of "reverse smuggling" of Heroin from Afghanistan that was routed through Africa and then shipped to India. The Indian authorities also shed light on the exploitation of young people from the northeastern regions by Nigerian gangs to serve as drug carriers.

It was revealed that Nigerians constitute a significant portion of all foreign individuals arrested in India for drug offences, accounting for 27 per cent of the total.

These discussions emphasize the need for international cooperation in the fight against the illegal drug trade and the protection of young and vulnerable individuals from being used as pawns in this dangerous game.

The Himachal Pradesh state police's NCB pointed out that the majority of Nigerian drug traffickers caught in Himachal Pradesh were operating from Delhi.

According to the police, Nigerian nationals from the capital city are actively involved in smuggling adulterated Heroin, known locally as **Chitta**, into Himachal Pradesh, leading to a significant increase in drug trafficking activities in the region.

The data also showed that the majority of drug peddlers in Himachal Pradesh are young people between the ages of 16 and 26.

The proliferation of Chitta, or adulterated Heroin, in Himachal Pradesh, is due to the operation of three distinct drug trafficking networks. The first is controlled by smugglers based in Punjab, the second by African criminal gangs, and the third originates from Uttar Pradesh.

The influx of Chitta has reached even remote, tourist-heavy areas such as Shimla, Kangra, Una, Sirmaur, and Solan. The problem is particularly dire in districts that share a border with Punjab.

In the hinterlands, the insidious tendrils of Chitta traffickers have reached and spread, necessitating a more fervent and proactive posture from the government in the face of this rapidly escalating crisis.

As the drug crisis continues to escalate, it becomes increasingly clear that government intervention is necessary to curb the spread of drug trafficking, especially in remote areas where traffickers have established a stronghold. In these tourist-heavy regions, the situation is particularly dire, and urgent action must be taken to put a stop to the trade of Chitta and other illegal drugs. The government must adopt a more proactive stance to tackle this growing problem before it becomes an even greater threat to public health and safety.

The high rate of unemployment in Nigeria, which has left over half of the country's labour force without proper employment or income, is causing some citizens to turn to drug trafficking as a means of making money. Despite government efforts to curb drug usage and impose strict punishments, drug trafficking remains a persistent problem in Nigeria, with smugglers becoming increasingly bold in their tactics.

In an effort to combat this problem, Nigeria has taken the step of sharing crucial intelligence regarding drug trafficking with India. This collaboration between the two nations demonstrates a commitment to a collective and global solution to the drug menace and serves as a beacon of hope for a more prosperous and drug-free future.

> The NCB has written to the Ministry of External Affairs and the Intelligence Bureau (IB) to address the issue of African nationals involved in drug trafficking activities in India.

The NCB has highlighted the difficulties encountered while dealing with such individuals and has requested the implementation of a travel ban or a stricter visa policy for African countries.

> In a shocking event in January 2023, Delhi Police officials were assaulted by a crowd of 100 African nationals who assisted three African nationals who were apprehended by the police for unlawfully living in India.

In recent years, the Mumbai Anti-Narcotics Cell and the NCB have arrested numerous African nationals in connection with drug trafficking activities. In 2021, around 43 African nationals were arrested, 40 of which were from Nigeria. Similarly, in 2019 and 2020, 25 Nigerians were arrested by the ANC in Mumbai alone.

Illegal Cannabis and Opium Cultivation

The CBN is the premier drug enforcement organization in charge of finding and eradicating illegal Cannabis and Opium cultivation, among many other important things.

> Recently, officers from the CBN demolished 1032 hectares (12,900 bighas) of illicit Cannabis (Ganja) production in one of Himachal Pradesh's largest destruction operations.

GPS coordinates were used to tag/mark the sensitive locations and drones were used for detection and surveillance of the illicit Cannabis (Ganja) cultivation areas which resulted in greater success of the entire operation.

CBN has carried out destruction operations in several states, including West Bengal, Jammu & Kashmir, Arunachal Pradesh, Manipur, and Uttarakhand, resulting in the elimination of nearly 25,000 hectares of illegal Opium and Cannabis growth throughout the years. In addition, CBN eradicated almost 3,600 hectares of Opium in Arunachal Pradesh between February and March 2022. The CBN intends to conduct similar illegal cultivation destruction operations throughout India in the future.

The government of Manipur has undertaken a huge campaign against illicit poppy farming on a gigantic scale. There have been 703 arrests, including five hill village heads, and the destruction of nearly 400 acres of poppy crops. Illicit cultivation of poppy is a significant issue in Ukhrul, Senapati, Kangpokpi, Kamjong, Churachandpur, and Tengnoupal.

Between 2017 and 2022, law enforcement authorities such as the Manipur Police eradicated around 18,000 acres of illegally cultivated poppy.

Illicit Opium and Heroin produced as a consequence of illegal poppy farming in Jammu and Kashmir eventually make their way into various marketplaces in Punjab.

Amritsar Customs destroyed the poppy crop illicitly grown at 23 locations in many J&K areas, including Pulwama, Shopian, and Anantnag.

> A grave concern that plagues our nation is the illicit cultivation of opiates and Cannabis.

It is a well-known fact that from each hectare of poppy fields, an average of 60 kg of illegal Opium is produced. Subsequently, this process yields around three to four kilos of pure Heroin, which may increase in a range from five to six kilos, depending on the extent of adulteration, cutting and dilution. It attracts an exorbitant international market price of five crore rupees per kilogram. In various states of our nation, including West Bengal, Jammu and Kashmir, Arunachal Pradesh, Manipur, and Uttarakhand, illicit poppy cultivation spans thousands of acres each year.

> Illicit cultivation of Cannabis is even more when compared to poppy.

It is no secret that drug traffickers have long-established ties with the widespread illegal cultivation in these states. The efficacy of state and central agencies in identifying and eliminating these illicit crops may not be significantly high. The proliferation of illicit cultivation is aided by numerous factors, and locally produced Heroin can be valued at a staggering thousand crore due to its surreptitious nature. This poses a grave threat to the well-being of our nation, and the youth are increasingly becoming victims of this drug epidemic. The Northeast states have been grappling with the pernicious effects of this issue for decades.

HEMP—STILL IN THE NASCENT STAGE

The proprietors of a café in Kozhikode were booked by the excise department. Kozhikode is a seaside city in Kerala. It was a prominent spice trading hub and is adjacent to Kappad Beach, where Portuguese navigator Vasco da Gama arrived in 1498.

Food samples were gathered by the authorities. The milkshakes were believed to include Ganja seeds in the form of oil. The seed oil was submitted to the Kozhikode regional chemical lab for examination, and a case was filed against the firm under NDPS Act.

> Most people can't quite put their finger on what distinguishes Cannabis, Ganja, Charas, Hashish, and Hemp from one another.

In layman's terms, they all originate from the same plant. Therein lies the resistance and stigma, not just in the minds of the general public but also, tragically, of the policymakers. While Ganja, also known as Marijuana or Weed, is formed from the dried flower buds of the Cannabis plant, bhang is a paste prepared by grinding together Cannabis leaves and stems. Charas, made by rubbing Cannabis flowers for hours (the longer, the better), is the most potent of the three.

Contrary to popular assumption, Cannabis is not entirely prohibited in India, although it is strictly regulated. Sections

8 and 10 of the NDPS Act empower state governments to license Cannabis growing for research and medicinal purposes. Section 14 also allows governments to issue general or specific orders allowing the cultivation of Cannabis solely for industrial and horticultural purposes.

> On November 15, 2021, FSSAI published a notice saying, "The hemp seed, hemp seed oil, and hemp seed flour shall be sold as food or used as an ingredient in a food for sale subject to complying requirements." This will cause a paradigm shift in how people see hemp.

So, milkshakes at the Kozhikode Café were getting an extra health boost with the addition of hemp seeds and oils!

The question now is, what is hemp?

In simple terms, both Marijuana and hemp are derived from the Cannabis plant, Cannabis Sativa L. However, they differ in the amount of the key psychoactive component that they contain. Hemp refers to Cannabis plants with a THC content of 0.3 per cent or less; Marijuana refers to plants with a THC content of 0.3 per cent or higher. THC concentration is important for both legal and policy reasons. Scientifically speaking, THC is the primary psychoactive ingredient of Cannabis and one of at least 113 total cannabinoids identified on the plant. When smoked, THC enters the circulation and goes to the brain, where it binds to naturally existing cannabinoid receptors sensors in the cerebral cortex, cerebellum, and basal ganglia. These are the areas of the brain that are in charge of thought, memory, pleasure, coordination, and movement. The higher the THC percentage, the deeper the impact on the brain and the greater the intoxication. If there is less THC, the influence on the brain will be insignificant.

> Uttarakhand has become the first state in India to give a hemp cultivation license.

It is allowed to cultivate hemp if it contains less than 0.3 per cent THC, and approval to cultivate it is granted subject to rules and regulations. The organization that wants to engage in this agricultural area may have to tread cautiously in uncharted territory. It is a road less travelled, thus it may hold many surprises.

Similarly, the Food Safety and Standards Authority of India (FSSAI) notification sets limits on how much moisture, fat, free fatty acids, THC, and CBD can be in hemp products. According to the notification, the amount of THC in any beverage from hemp seeds can't be more than 0.2 mg/kg. Also, the total amount of THC in any other food for sale that is made of hemp seed or seed products cannot be more than 5 mg/kg. The notification also asserts that the level of cannabidiol (CBD) in any food made from hemp seed or products made from hemp seed shall not be more than 75 mg/kg. Nonetheless, there are several caveats despite FSSAI's declaration that hemp is a food.

> The hemp sector in India is still in its nascent stage, due to rising consumer demand and public interest in hemp products, the future looks promising.

The entrance of hemp seeds into FSSAI will for sure stir consumer awareness, further encouraging the expansion of the Indian hemp sector. Hemp, according to expert predictions, will reach its full disruptive potential in a decade. However, to what extent an industry within the economy will become commercial essentially depends and hinges on the policies of the government, the transparency in the system and the priorities of the key player and stake holders in the sector.

The Chemistry and Economics of Drugs

PRECURSORS AND PRE-PRECURSORS

There are immense complexities and challenges in controlling the production of synthetic and semi-synthetic drugs. The equation "no chemicals" equals "no drugs" may seem simple in theory, but in reality, it's not practical. This is because the chemicals that are used to make these drugs also have legitimate uses for important products and banning them altogether is not feasible. Thus, the international community must strike a balance between preventing the illegal use of these substances and ensuring that they remain available for legal purposes. This balance is the underlying principle of international drug control treaties.

> The chemical Acetic Anhydride is a simple example of the challenges in controlling precursor chemicals.

While it is an essential ingredient for manufacturing paracetamol, it is also used to process Heroin from Opium. Banning the chemical altogether would prevent the production of legitimate and important products like paracetamol, but not controlling its distribution could lead to the illegal manufacture of drugs like Heroin. Therefore, a balanced approach is needed to regulate the availability of precursor chemicals for legal use while preventing their diversion for illicit purposes. This illustrates the complexities involved in drug control and the need for a nuanced approach.

The international drug control treaties have identified and categorized many chemicals that have the potential to be used in the illicit manufacture of drugs. Countries that have signed these treaties work to regulate the distribution of these precursors to prevent them from falling into the hands of drug traffickers.

However, despite these efforts, new challenges arise in the form of non-scheduled chemicals, designer precursors, and pre-precursors that can be used as substitutes for controlled precursors.

These emerging alternatives to regulated precursors make it difficult to keep up with the changing landscape of drug manufacture and trafficking. Therefore, there is a continuous need to monitor and adapt to new developments in the illicit drug trade to effectively combat it.

The International Narcotics Control Board (INCB) has reported a significant drop in the amount of ephedrine and pseudoephedrine seized in 2019 for the illicit production of Methamphetamine, down to only 5.7 tons from 40 tons in 2018. This highlights the shift towards the use of possible alternatives for such substances, such as the ephedra plant, which was also reported as a source of Methamphetamine production in China and Afghanistan. In contrast, seizures of potassium permanganate, the traditional precursor of Cocaine, remained stable, but there is evidence of a spread in the use of alternative Cocaine precursors, such as potassium manganate and sodium permanganate, outside of South America. These findings demonstrate the constant need for monitoring and adapting to emerging trends in the illicit drug trade to effectively combat it.

In 2020, several significant seizures of acetic anhydride were reported across different countries. Authorities in Iran seized a consignment of 15 tons of acetic anhydride misdeclared as paint and bound for Afghanistan. Pakistan also reported two seizures of acetic anhydride, with one consignment misdeclared as acetic acid and the other suspected to have originated in China.

> A few years ago, a large quantity of 7000 litres of acetic anhydride was seized from a warehouse near Ahmedabad.

The drug traffickers were planning to clandestinely send the said consignment to the Rajasthan-Pakistan border for Heroin production. Myanmar reported its largest seizure of more than 4,000 litres of acetic anhydride in almost two decades and later seized almost 10,300 litres from a truck, along with hydrochloric acid and caffeine. Most of the precursors smuggled into Myanmar in 2020 were reported to have come from China and transported to illicit manufacturing sites in the border area, where governance was limited due to armed conflicts. These incidents highlight the continued challenge of preventing the diversion of precursor chemicals for illicit drug production, particularly in areas with limited governance and ongoing conflicts.

The Indian government tightened controls over two fentanyl precursors, ANPP (4-anilino-N-phenethyl-4-piperidine) and NPP (N-phenethyl-4-piperidone), in August 2020, after instances of diversion of domestically manufactured ANPP for trafficking to Mexico. India was the largest exporter of NPP. As per reports, two clandestine ketamine laboratories in India in 2019 and 2020 were dismantled in Bangalore and Chennai.

Cooks, Kitchens, and Recipes

Meth labs are makeshift laboratories where individuals produce and synthesize Methamphetamine, commonly referred to as Meth. These labs are popping up at an alarming rate to meet the high demand for the highly addictive drug. They can be found in homes, apartments, garages, and even hotels, with some individuals converting their automobiles into labs. Meth labs are often located in secluded areas to avoid detection. The production of Meth involves using one of two main Methods, one based on ephedrine or pseudoephedrine and the other using BMK. The starting materials for these Methods can be bulk powders, medicinal products, or designer precursors. Those who produce Methamphetamine in Meth labs are often referred to as "cooks" due to the nature of the production process, which involves cooking and synthesizing chemicals, and the term "kitchens" is often used by drug traffickers to refer to Meth labs because they are frequently located in kitchens or other areas of homes where cooking typically takes place. With high-profit margins, Meth has become one of the favourite drugs for drug traffickers. Meth is a highly addictive drug that acts as a potent CNS stimulant and affects the brain's neurotransmitters, resulting in the release of high levels of dopamine.

The cooks are constantly in search of novel methods for the synthesis of drugs. They explore new formulas—'recipes'. The whole purpose is to bypass the routine methods and do away with the need for known precursors.

> There are many reports where the synthesis of various drugs using pre-precursors or newer chemicals is observed.

This can make their job easier and safer, as with the use of pre-precursors or other untested chemicals, they may be able to avoid detection by law enforcement agencies.

> Recently many such cooking centres were busted in Kerala. A cooking centre run by Nigerians in one of the posh localities of Greater Noida was busted too.

The COVID pandemic has led to a major shift in the way drug trafficking takes place around the world. We have now seen the emergence of innovative techniques for drug trafficking, as well as new methods for drug synthesis. This includes the blending and mixing of substances with newer components, the use of pre-precursors and alternative chemicals, and the adoption of new technologies for secretive communication. Drug markets are getting more and more complicated these days. Along with traditional drugs like Cannabis, Cocaine, and Heroin, hundreds of synthetic drugs have emerged, many of which are not under international control. There has also been a rapid increase in the non-medical use of prescription drugs.

Every year, around 500 NPS are discovered in markets. These all are the result of new recipes synthesised by the cooks in their kitchens.

THE PHARMA NEXUS—A WELL-OILED NETWORK

India is one of the largest producers of generic medicines in the world. However, a single dirty fish can spoil the whole pond.

> Many drug pharma syndicates misuse their facilities for a quick buck.

One 100 ml bottle of codeine-based cough syrup (CBCS) is equivalent to a 30 mg Morphine pill. Codeine is a pro-drug generated from Opium that is converted to Morphine in the liver. Many of these OTC cough syrups include codeine, an opioid that may lead to addiction. In fact, very few of us are aware that the substance is an addictive narcotic, similar to Heroin.

> From Gujarat to Tripura and from Jammu and Kashmir to Tamil Nadu, the menace of CBCS abuse has been growing over the years despite a crackdown on it from time to time.

What's more, there is rampant cross-border smuggling to Bangladesh and Nepal.

Anti-narcotic agencies have always been on their toe. But the volumes of such transactions are so huge that it seems only a small fraction of the same is seized. In the recent past many seizures were affected.

- 5,920 bottles of cough syrup were seized by the police in Bolangir, Odisha.
- 9,500 bottles of codeine-containing cough syrups were seized near Guwahati.
- The BSF seized over 33,536 bottles of Phensedyl from smugglers along the South Bengal front during the lockdown period.
- The BSF in a joint operation with customs officials seized 21,400 Phensedyl bottles from four trucks.
- One lakh bottle of CBCS worth ₹1.76 crore was seized by DRI officials. The DRI claimed that they had busted a major racket engaged in smuggling cough syrups into Northeast India from Uttar Pradesh, Jammu, and Madhya Pradesh.
- State-run laboratories in West Bengal found twice the amount of codeine (21.37 mg/5ml dosage instead of 10 mg/5ml) in a batch of Phensedyl bottles.
- Two drug wholesalers for smuggling two lakh bottles of a popular cough syrup sold by a multinational pharmaceutical giant.
- 10,000 CBCS bottles were seized in the Sirmaur district, Himachal Pradesh.
- 42,000 bottles of safe codeine phosphate cough syrup, worth ₹47 lakh were seized in Gujarat.

It is learned that NCB has seized more than 9.5 lakh bottles of CBCS over the past few years.

The Indian government's plan to ban codeine-based cough syrups to prevent their rampant misuse was strongly opposed by the pharma industry.

The Indian Drug Manufacturer Association (IDMA) opposed the proposal for a ban, stating that cough syrups are necessary for managing coughs in various medical conditions.

It's not only CBCS which are illegally diverted into the market for drug abuse. There are many other pharmaceutical drugs on the same lines.

The agencies seized a significant amount of illicitly diverted pharmaceutical drugs, valued at around rupees five crore, and arrested one person in connection to an interstate drug trafficking syndicate operating in Mumbai. The drugs seized include 1,32,000 alprazolam tablets and 2,400 CBCS bottles, which are commonly abused by a large section of the population. The syndicate was found to be procuring drugs from UP-Bihar-based local suppliers through inter-state transport companies. Many fake medical/pharma entities were created for this purpose.

A drug-pharma syndicate was recently busted, which was running an illegal drug trade worth more than ₹100 crore from a wholesale drug trading company in Baddi, Himachal Pradesh.

The company obtained NDPS permission for formulations for legal sale from the narcotic control bureau but diverted them for illegal use as sedatives and hypnotics. In violation of NDPS Act rules, the accused used fake sales bills to sell NDPS drugs to a mandi-based wholesale drug dealer and transport them to other states. Many shipments were delivered to Rajasthan and other parts of the country.

A Hyderabad-based pharma firm was raided; they were illegally re-exporting 25,000 kg of tramadol to Pakistan, despite having permission to export to Denmark, Germany, and Malaysia only. The company also reported a discrepancy in acetic anhydride, a precursor substance used to produce Heroin. The managing director, associate vice president, and three other employees of the company were arrested. The widespread availability of information about production methods and the high profit margins associated with it have made the synthetic drug mephedrone or MD a popular choice among traffickers in India. Recently, 225 kg of mephedrone valued at ₹1,125 crore was seized from a makeshift plant near Vadodara.

> The pharma nexus with the drug mafias is a well-oiled network of people, top officials from pharma firms, clearing and forwarding agents in states, drug warehouse owners and influential people, engaged in this illegal trade where the demand for production is kept high in contrast to actual consumption. The experts and concerned authorities need to conduct an in-depth evidence-based analytical study to find out the actual demand for the above-mentioned pharma drugs and the overall production, which will expose the whole nexus.

A System Failure—Unbecoming of an Officer

Certain officers of the NCB are under scrutiny for their handling of the recent cruise drug case, which has raised concerns about the quality of the investigation. The agency faced criticism from a large section of society over the shoddy investigation, which could erode public trust in the agency and create a perception that affluent and prominent individuals can evade consequences. A vigilance action was thus proposed, and many officers were shunted.

While anti-narcotic officers at state and central levels have worked diligently to establish a drug-free society, previous instances of misconduct by some officers have brought shame to their departments.

A former Zonal Director of the NCB in Chandigarh was sentenced to 15 years in jail for possessing and attempting to sell drugs. The case has raised questions about the unethical practices within government agencies tasked with eliminating the drug problem, as the distinction between smugglers and law enforcement officials has become blurred. The officer was accused of secretly stealing drugs from storage facilities and selling them in cities such as Amritsar, Ferozepur, and Jammu. The theft was discovered when some of his colleagues became suspicious of his shady recoveries and reported their concerns. Court documents show that he and some members of his team adulterated the stolen drugs and sold them.

> The prosecution claims that the NCB officer mixed slaked lime into drugs and kept the pure contraband for himself while serving as the NCB Zonal Director.

His subordinate staff was aware of the theft and the cash seized from smugglers was distributed among them. It is also alleged that he gave 10 kg of Heroin to a drug smuggler from Jammu.

The arrest of a Punjab police official and three others for allegedly possessing drugs worth 20 crore rupees has once again shed light on the growing drug trade in the region. According to sources, the NCB conducted an operation that led to the seizure of 25 kg of Methamphetamine, which has an estimated international market value of ₹20 crore. The wrestler, who has won the prestigious Arjuna Award, was among the individuals held in the operation. This case raises concerns about the extent of the drug trade in the area and the need for more effective measures to combat it.

A recent investigation has uncovered that the prominent Israeli drug lord in Goa was supplied drugs by some foreign national individuals, including Russians and Africans. An Israeli drug dealer also confirmed that he received drugs from a corrupt police officer in Goa, which had been infiltrated.

Despite attempts to hide the theft, a large quantity of 24 kg of Hashish went missing from the anti-drug storage, with the Goa minister offering the unlikely explanation that the drugs were "eaten by white ants".

A few years ago, a court clerk tasked with the supervision of a *malkhana* in Mumbai was exposed for engaging in an unscrupulous act of pilfering confiscated drugs from the storage facility. The individual would replace the stolen contraband with other substances, in a cunning attempt to conceal their thievery. Upon being confronted with the evidence of their wrongdoing, the clerk offered a feeble excuse that the drugs had been consumed by rodents.

In Bengaluru, an inspector and a sub-inspector were suspended for diluting charges against two constables who were caught in a drug peddling case.

Meanwhile, the Special Task Force and District Police in Punjab have taken decisive action against corruption within their ranks by initiating 114 criminal cases against 148 police personnel and departmental inquiries against 61 individuals from April 2017 to April 30, 2020.

These investigations aimed to uncover the connection between police department employees and drug trafficking.

Three police officers were suspended in Odisha's Boudh district for releasing a Cannabis smuggler and keeping the recovered Marijuana for themselves. They are believed to have been in collaboration with drug smugglers, collecting money for the transport of the banned substance, and using their official quarters as storage for the contraband.

> In Arunachal Pradesh, a police sub-inspector was arrested for drug trafficking and possession of drugs.

In Kashmir's Kupwara district, 17 people, including five police officers, were arrested on charges of being part of a drug trafficking cartel using drugs sourced from Pakistan. The bust reveals the direct involvement of Pakistan in smuggling drugs into Kashmir through their henchmen and terrorist handlers. Similarly, in Punjab, an inspector was arrested by the special task force for drug trafficking, and a large quantity of drugs, arms, and ammunition was seized from his official quarters.

These cases serve as a reminder of the ongoing issue of corruption within law enforcement agencies and the importance of taking strong measures to combat it. The system needs to be made crash-proof. Exemplary and stringent action against these officers is the need of the hour.

Bushy Plant to "Shisha": The Dangerous Industry

Ephedra—Somlata—The Afghan Angle

The production and trafficking of Methamphetamine (Meth) are skyrocketing in Afghanistan, making it one of the fastest-growing illicit drugs in the country. This is due to the extensive growth of the ephedra plant, commonly known as *'Oman' or 'bandak'*, in the central highlands. The ephedra plant provides an ample and affordable source of ephedrine, which is crucial for producing Methamphetamine.

Typically, most of the Meth produced globally is derived from synthetic ephedrine found in cough and cold medicines but obtaining enough of this chemical to support production is time-consuming and expensive. On the other hand, ephedra is plentiful in Afghanistan and its unregulated harvesting and processing make it a tempting option for drug makers.

The discovery of the wild ephedra bush in Afghanistan has sparked a dangerous industry, positioning the country as a potential player in the global synthetic drug trade.

The ephedra plant, which grows in central and northern Afghanistan, contains ephedrine, a stimulant commonly used in decongestants and weight loss pills and as a key ingredient in making Crystal Meth. The availability of this plant has led to a surge in Crystal Meth use and dependence, both in urban and rural areas. The plant's growth in the central and northern regions of Afghanistan has caused makeshift Meth labs to proliferate, providing a cheap source of low-quality Crystal Meth. The ease of production has attracted those seeking quick profits, increasing abuse and the spread of addiction and related health problems.

The origin of how Afghan producers learned to extract ephedrine from the ephedra plant remains unknown, with reports suggesting that Iran and China could have been the source. One theory proposes that Iranian Meth producers shared their knowledge with Afghan producers during a crackdown on Meth production in Iran during the mid-2010s. However, the true origin remains a mystery, known only to the producers themselves. Over time, producers have become more skilled in selecting and processing high-quality 'Oman', now capable of producing 17 pounds of Meth from 1,000 pounds of dried ephedra. The Opium and Heroin trade in Afghanistan is estimated to be worth $6.6 billion per year, according to a 2018 report from the United Nations Office on Drugs and Crime (UNODC).

Afghanistan has thus become a major producer and supplier of low-cost ephedrine and Methamphetamine, with its producers selling their products at a fraction of the production cost in Southeast Asia. The Taliban, who have long-standing experience in processing and transporting Heroin, control almost all of Afghanistan's narcotics and drug distribution networks, which places Afghanistan in a strong position to be a key player in the global synthetic illicit drug trade.

According to the UNODC, Afghanistan has quickly emerged as a significant producer and supplier of ephedrine and Methamphetamine, largely due to the abundance of the ephedra plant. The chemicals required for production, including iodine, red phosphorus, and sulfuric acid, are readily accessible and unregulated in their country.

> Drug mafias in Afghanistan have taken advantage of the ephedra plant for Methamphetamine production.

In addition to ephedrine, which can be obtained from the plant, the process only requires a few basic chemicals, kitchen glassware, and a gas burner, making the production of Methamphetamine easy and cheap. The high yield and low cost of the production process from the ephedra plant in Afghanistan give them a competitive edge in the global illicit drug market.

The conversion of ephedra into ephedrine involves soaking the dried plant in a mixture of gasoline, water, salt, and caustic soda for 24 hours, then heating the solution with salt, sulfuric acid, and xylene, producing a residue that is ephedrine. This substance can be sold or further processed into Meth. The Taliban, with its extensive experience in the drug trade, controls most of Afghanistan's drug distribution networks, allowing the country to penetrate international markets through established and new drug-trafficking routes. This is evident in the seizures of over 3,000 kg of Meth with Afghan markings in countries such as Pakistan, Mozambique, Australia, Indonesia, and Sri Lanka.

The production of Crystal Methamphetamine, also known as "shisha" in Afghanistan has become a thriving industry. The key ingredient, ephedrine, is extracted from the abundant wild ephedra bush, which grows in the central and northern regions of the country. This plant has breathed life into a new and alarming trade, positioning Afghanistan as a potential major player in the global synthetic drug market. The extraction of ephedrine is a relatively simple process; however, the production of Methamphetamine requires a higher level of skill and knowledge.

> The potential for production is vast, with some sources estimating that a single valley in Ghazni could produce up to 2,500 metric tons of ephedra in one season, translating to 8 to 25 metric tons of Methamphetamine.

The abundance of Oman in the district of Taywara, with its 1400 villages situated at elevations of 2500 meters or higher, makes it an ideal location for its cultivation. A single 15-metric-ton truck of Oman can yield up to 265 kg of Methamphetamine.

The low cost of production in Afghanistan, thanks to the use of the ephedra plant, has reduced the cost of producing the drug by 50 per cent. The rapid growth of the industry has raised concerns among officials about the widespread availability of low-quality Crystal Meth. The exact origin of how local producers learned to extract ephedrine from ephedra remains a mystery, with reports suggesting Iran and China as possible sources. The Opium and Heroin trade in Afghanistan is estimated to be worth around $6.6 billion per year, and it is believed that the Methamphetamine trade could soon rival it.

While the cultivation of Oman has the potential to bring economic growth to the region, it also poses significant challenges. The illegal production of Methamphetamine can lead to environmental damage, organized crime, violence, and addiction among the local population, with negative impacts on social and health issues, stability, and vulnerability to crime and conflict.

To mitigate these risks, the authorities need to take a comprehensive approach to the issue, including addressing the demand for illegal drugs and improving the economic opportunities for communities in the region. The international community should also provide support for Afghan authorities to tackle the issue, including funding for drug education and prevention programmes, as well as supporting the development of alternative crops and livelihoods for the people of Afghanistan.

Interestingly, ephedra is a plant that is native to China and India, and it has been used for medicinal purposes for centuries. It is a low-growing evergreen shrub with small scaly leaves, and it was commonly used to treat a variety of ailments, including colds, headaches, and coughing. However, in 2004, the US FDA banned the sale of dietary supplements that contained ephedrine alkaloids, which are stimulant compounds found in some species of ephedra.

Ephedra gerardiana, also known as Soma, Somlata, or divine Somaras in India, is a species of ephedra that grows in the Alpine Himalayas from Kashmir to Sikkim, Chamba, and Ladakh.

This plant has been used for medicinal purposes for a long time. The possibilities of illegal shipment of this unique, Himalayan-grown bushy plant and its usage in the production of Meth cannot be ruled out, since several drug cartels of Afghan Iranian origin could well have explored it. The state as well as the central anti-narcotic agencies need to look into this aspect and ensure that there is no misuse of this plant in the illicit drug trade.

THE ECONOMICS OF DRUGS: MONEY MATTERS

It is estimated that the illegal drug trade accounts for around one per cent of the world economy, with an annual value of at least one trillion dollars, or nearly eighty lakh crore of Indian rupees. Multiple studies have suggested that the illicit drug trade has a major influence on the economy. Even though it is impossible to ascertain the precise quantity of the illegal drug trade, these figures are just approximations. It is by far one of the most profitable and lucrative businesses, and that is why, despite the best efforts of many governments who have declared war on drugs, it is continually growing and spreading its tentacles.

Like any other business, the illicit drug trade follows a supply chain that extends from the cultivation of crops to the distribution of the final product to the end consumer. The primary difference in the illicit drug trade is the high level of risk involved at every stage of the supply chain. Profit margins can vary depending on the segment of the supply chain that faces the highest risk. The price of the end product reaching the last person in the chain will reflect these factors.

To provide a simple example, the cost of a kilogram of illicit raw Opium paid to the farmer may sometimes be lower than the cost of just a few grams of white Heroin sold to a drug addict during a rave party.

There are significant risks and uncertainties associated with the illegal drug trade, including law enforcement crackdowns, variations in demand, and the possibility of violent rivalry amongst drug trafficking groups. Consequently, drug markups are highest at the retail level, when drugs are sold directly to consumers. This enables drug pushers and peddlers to compensate for their significant risks and probable losses.

As the most visible and accessible segment of the drug supply chain, retailers are especially susceptible to law enforcement actions. Due to the illicit and uncontrolled nature of the drug trade, they also work with a customer that may be unpredictable and changeable, exposing them to risk or financial loss. Consequently, drug mafias may charge substantial markups to compensate for the risks and expenses involved with operating in the illegal drug market. Apart from this adding cutting agents or adulterating the drugs is a common modus operandi adopted by the drug peddlers, to increase their profit margins.

Money Launderers and Hawala Operators

The illicit drug trade operates both locally and internationally, much like any other business. However, the international drug trade is largely controlled by drug mafias who are often involved in various other criminal activities, such as illegal arms trade, support for terrorist organizations, and money laundering. These drug mafias have significant power and influence, and their illegal activities can have wide-ranging impacts on both society and the economy.

Money launderers and hawala operators have close-knit relations with drug traffickers. As drugs are bought and sold, the profits generated from these illegal activities must be cleaned and moved out of the country or parked in some business entity. Research has shown that drug money is typically laundered through investments in real estate and gold, which are common ways of hiding illicit funds. Money laundering often involves the exploitation of legitimate services and professionals like accountants, lawyers, and estate agents. These individuals can act as intermediaries and use their expertise to facilitate the movement and storage of criminal money, create complex structures, generate fake invoices-transport documents and shell companies to conceal ownership and disseminate funds.

> Money is a crucial aspect when it comes to drugs. Money laundering is one of the important arms of drug trafficking. If the money trail can be traced, the drug mafias can be exposed. Lakhs of crore exchange hands in the drug trade.

The funds need to be transferred to the mafias who supply the drugs. In the instances where the drugs are being smuggled into India, the money must ultimately flow back to the suppliers. Hawala operators play a very vital role here. The hawala operators manage to transfer money in any nation on the globe. Cash is handed over to an operator A in India, who intimates his associate hawala operator in the respective country and ultimately, the supplier receives the money. Thousands of crore are exchanged through hawala daily and the enforcement agencies world over have not been able to plug this.

> According to studies, the worldwide drug trade, including illicit drug trafficking, generates over $1 trillion in revenue annually, which is equivalent to more than 80 lakh crore per year.

Currently, India comprises over 17 per cent of the global population and has seen a significant increase in drug trafficking and consumption in the past decade.

> Even a small and modest percentage, just two to three per cent, of the global drug trade can result in almost 2.5 lakh crore rupees per year, which equates to approximately 680 crore per day.

The numbers are staggering and highlight the potential for hawala transactions, money laundering, and an illegal economy associated with drug trafficking in India.

Another modus operandi is the undervaluation of exports or overvaluation of imports. The differential payment is used to pay the drug suppliers in the respective country. In both these scenarios, the customs departments have not been able to get much success in unearthing these transactions.

Law enforcement officers have a really tough time unearthing such financial issues and drug money connections. The ₹21,000 crore Mudra Port Heroin case, which the NIA is investigating, has opened Pandora's box and a trail of similar fraudulent and dubious financial records.

Section 7

The Global Drug Scenario

All Eyes on Afghanistan, Iran, and Pakistan

The UNODC Report 2022 sheds light on significant developments in the global drug market. Cocaine production has hit an all-time high, while seizures of Amphetamine and Methamphetamine have surged. These drugs are now being trafficked to new and more vulnerable regions, fueling harmful patterns of drug use that have likely worsened amid the COVID-19 pandemic. The youth are particularly susceptible, with more of them using drugs than previous generations.

Trafficking by sea, particularly in shipping containers, has expanded significantly, with nearly 90 per cent of globally seized Cocaine in 2021 being transported via this mode.

The future of the global opiate market hinges on the situation in Afghanistan, which accounted for a staggering 86 per cent of illicit Opium production in 2021. Global Opium production has been on an upward trajectory over the past two decades.

Methamphetamine use and production have surpassed "traditional" markets in East and South-East Asia, with a marked rise in seizures in Afghanistan and wider regional trafficking.

Synthetic drug trafficking, particularly ATS, has seen faster growth than plant-based drugs over the past two decades, with a sharp increase in global seizures of ATS over the previous decade.

> Methamphetamine seizures have increased five-fold, Amphetamine four-fold, and Ecstasy three-fold.

As chemical control measures are implemented, the precursors used in synthetic drug production are rapidly evolving, leading to the emergence of pre-precursors and "designer precursors."

In today's globalized world, shipping lanes play a crucial role in facilitating international trade. However, this has also opened up opportunities for transnational organized crime groups and terrorists to smuggle prohibited drugs, weapons of mass destruction, and other illegal goods through shipping containers. With less than two per cent of shipping containers being screened, monitoring this vast global trade has become increasingly difficult.

Moreover, the rise of darknet technologies has made it easier for individuals to anonymously access crypto markets and exploit standard postal and commercial shipping services. This coupled with the use of sophisticated concealment measures, corruption, limited resources, and a lack of trust and coordination between government departments as well as enforcement agencies and the private sector, poses a serious threat. The drug mafias exploit all such weak links in the chain.

Drug traffickers have been found to use shipping containers to smuggle drugs by concealing them in legitimate cargo with low prices and similar appearance.

> The Drug Enforcement Agency (DEA) has detected several cases where drugs were hidden in declared goods, such as semi-processed talc stones, apple and pomegranate juice, and rock salt. The majority of these cases were traced back to Bandar Abbas Port in Iran, which is on the southern route of Heroin trafficking from Afghanistan.

These new and innovative methods of drug trafficking pose serious challenges for law enforcement agencies worldwide.

A glance at some of such detections and seizures done by DRI gives in insight into the magnitude of the issue.

On April 20, 2021, a shipment of teak wood from Panama was intercepted at the port of Tuticorin, India. The cargo contained 300 kg of Cocaine, which had been cleverly hidden inside the container carrying the wood. The narcotics were smuggled in a way that made them almost undetectable, and it was only through the diligent efforts of the authorities that the drugs were uncovered.

Another interception occurred on June 23, 2021, when a shipment of liquorice roots from Iran was seized at the port of Nhava Sheva in India. The cargo was found to contain 293 kg of Heroin, which had been concealed inside the liquorice roots. This was yet another example of how drug traffickers use innocent-looking goods as cover to smuggle narcotics.

In September 2021, a shipment of semi-processed talc stones from Afghanistan was loaded at the Port of Bandar Abbas, Iran and was imported to Mundra, India. The consignment declared as talc stones, concealed 2988 kg of Heroin in the middle layer of some of the jumbo bags in between the top and bottom layers of the declared goods. NIA took the investigation and dozens of arrests were made including many foreigners.

On October 4, 2021, a consignment of mustard seed oil (ground nut oil) was shipped from Bandar Abbas (Iran), Afghanistan, to Nhava Sheva, India. The shipment was found to contain 25 kg of Heroin concealed inside packets hidden inside oil cans.

In February 2022, a shipment of rock salt was loaded at the Port of Bandar Abbas (Iran) and imported to ICD Tughlaq Abad, India. The consignment declared as rock salt, concealed 34.7 kg of Heroin. The drug was hidden inside the consignment of rock salt.

On March 8, 2022, a shipment of apple and pomegranate juice was loaded at the Port of Bandar Abbas (Iran) and imported to ICD Tughlaq Abad, India. The consignment declared as juice, concealed 2.4 kg of Heroin inside it.

In March 2023, the ICG apprehended an Iranian boat with five Iranian crew in Indian waters, near Okha, carrying 61 kg Heroin worth ₹ 425 crore.

These incidents highlight the length that drug traffickers will go to conceal their illegal activities and the importance of constant vigilance by law enforcement agencies.

> **The majority of the drugs were smuggled from Afghanistan.**

Nevertheless, it is a matter of considerable concern that despite the most sincere and diligent efforts put forth by agencies, achieving a 100 per cent success rate is a near-impossible feat. The sheer magnitude of marine traffic and millions of tons of import consignments and containers arriving at diverse ports throughout the country renders it nearly unfeasible to entirely extinguish the scourge of drug trafficking.

Indian Ocean—An Ocean of Drugs

"Narcotics trafficking on the "merry-time" route poses a significant maritime challenge."

The Information Fusion Centre-Indian Ocean Region (IFRC-IOR), an Indian Navy initiative, recorded 757 incidents of contraband smuggling in the maritime domain in 2021, with drug smuggling being the most frequently reported type, accounting for 50 per cent of the total incidents. Of these, 376 were drug smuggling incidents, resulting in 457 drug seizures. The major types of drugs seized were cannabinoids, Amphetamine-Type Substances (ATS) such as Methamphetamine, and opioids like Heroin. The centre recorded an average monthly count of 31 drug seizures in the IOR in 2021, revealing regional manufacturing hubs and seaborne smuggling routes.

Drug trafficking in the Indian Ocean region remains a significant challenge, with a variety of methods used, including transhipment via dhows or small boats and concealment in containerized cargo. Criminal networks often use merchant vessels to transport drugs, either by concealing them within the vessel or by having the crew carry the drugs.

Transhipment using dhows or small boats is a common method of smuggling drugs, as it allows traffickers to quickly transfer the drugs from one vessel to another to avoid detection by law enforcement. Concealment in containerized cargo is also a popular method, as it allows smugglers to hide the drugs among legitimate goods being shipped overseas. Other methods of drug smuggling include "dead drops" in remote locations, where drugs are hidden for later pickup; buoys with GPS-fixed locations, which allow for the drugs to be easily retrieved; ditching the drugs at sea for later pickup or for the drugs to float ashore; and concealing the drugs under or attached to navigational buoys.

The "smack track" or "hash highway" refers to the Heroin and Hashish smuggling routes that originate from the Makran Coast or North Arabian Sea and are commonly referred to as the "Southern Route". However, traffickers are altering their routes in an effort to avoid patrols by warships.

The packaging of illicit drugs plays a significant role in drug trafficking, with traffickers using unique methods and branding to distinguish their products and establish a reputation for quality and reliability. In the western Indian Ocean region, Hashish and Cannabis are often packaged in large bales, while synthetic drugs are packaged in a distinctive manner that identifies their branding. The COVID-19 pandemic had impacted the resources and operations of law enforcement agencies, making it harder for them to effectively monitor and intercept drug smuggling activities.

The increasing demand for drugs such as Captagon in West Asia has prompted authorities to step up their efforts to combat drug trafficking. The UNODC has reported that trafficking routes for Captagon and other synthetic drugs in the region have become more sophisticated, with criminal networks using various modes of transport, including air, sea, and land, to smuggle the drugs to their markets. Despite these efforts, the challenge remains, as the criminal networks involved in drug trafficking are often well-equipped and highly organized, making it difficult for authorities to stop the flow of illicit drugs.

Recently, there has been a surge in the interdiction of "stateless" dhows operating in the Northern Arabian Sea by warships under the Combined Maritime Forces (CMF) umbrella. These vessels have a clear connection to Pakistan and are being used as part of the marine transportation component of the state-supported drug trade run by Taliban-linked drug lords in collaboration with Pakistani cartels. The crew members of these dhows, who are mostly Pakistani and occasionally Iranian, deliberately hide their identity by not carrying proper identity documents.

These drug-smuggling voyages begin from small coves and harbours along the Makran coast, the coastal region of Baluchistan in southeastern Iran and southwestern Pakistan, which spans across Pakistan and Iran. The smugglers often do not fly the flag of any nation while at sea, making it difficult for law enforcement agencies to identify the vessels and their origin. This "grey zone" in international maritime law has been exploited by Pakistan's deep state for many decades to run a massive drug and terrorism-based enterprise.

The impact of the pandemic on Pakistan's economy, along with cuts to its security and intelligence agency budgets, may have contributed to an increase in drug smuggling along the established maritime routes in the Indian Ocean. Pakistan's intelligence agency, the Inter-Services Intelligence (ISI), has been involved in the Afghanistan-based Heroin trade for many years, using the profits to fund subversive activities in India. This approach has been successful, and the deep state has sought to extend its narco-terror activities along its international border and Line of Control with India.

In 2021, the Indian Navy and Coast Guard detected and intercepted several fishing vessels that were suspected of transporting illicit drugs off India's west coast.

The seizures revealed significant amounts of narcotics. Pakistan's thriving drug trade has a negative impact on the entire South Asian region. Sri Lanka and the Maldives are two of the major destinations for drug shipments originating from the Makran coast in Pakistan. An investigation by India's NCB found that a drug trafficking ring operated by Pakistani drug lords jailed in Sri Lanka has been pushing drugs into India through the sea route using couriers from Sri Lanka and the Maldives. The drug network is believed to span Afghanistan, Pakistan, Iran, Sri Lanka, the Maldives, Australia, and India. The dire state of the Pakistani economy, the ease of recruiting poor fishermen from coastal areas as couriers, well-established supply chains between Afghanistan and the Makran coast, and a network of overseas collaborators make drug trafficking a highly lucrative enterprise for the Pakistani authorities. In the last 18 months, Indian Costal Guards (ICG), in coordination with Gujarat ATS, has apprehended eight foreign vessels in the Arabian Sea and seized 407 kg narcotics worth ₹ 2355 crore.

The Indian Ocean awash with illegal drugs

The IFC-IOR (Information Fusion Centre-Indian Ocean Region) was established by the Indian Navy in Gurugram on December 22, 2018, to enhance maritime safety and security in the Indian Ocean Region.

> The centre also hosts International Liaison Officers (ILOs) from 11 partner nations, including Australia, France, Japan, Maldives, Mauritius, Myanmar, Sri Lanka, Seychelles, Singapore, the United Kingdom, and the United States of America.

The aim is to facilitate better coordination, streamline information sharing, and provide timely inputs to enhance maritime security in the region.

Over several months in 2022, numerous cases were observed of illegal drugs across Indian Ocean international waters. From the Bay of Bengal to the Gulf of Oman and from Palk Bay to the Arabian Sea, drugs flow like water in the Indian Ocean. Multiple naval and coastal forces from different nations made hundreds of successful seizures, working tirelessly to prevent the proliferation of these illegal substances.

Nevertheless, it is quite possible that these efforts represent only a fraction of the overall problem, with much more of the illegal drug trade remaining beneath the surface, it may be just the tip of an iceberg and the major part is hidden like the bulk of an iceberg.

The enormity of this operation underscores the deep-rooted and ubiquitous nature of this illicit trade, which persists despite ongoing efforts to eradicate it.

A few of the incidents in 2022 based on the IFRC-IOR data plainly shows that the Indian Ocean is a sea of drug trafficking and gives an insight into the gravity and magnitude of the problem.

Crystal Methamphetamine (Ice) seizures

On June 25, in the Bay of Bengal off the coast of Myanmar, authorities seized 1,000 kg of Crystal Methamphetamine (Ice) with a value of USD 13,429,460 (equivalent to ₹110 crore).

A month later, on July 25, Indonesian authorities intercepted 11 kg of Methamphetamine in the Java Sea.

On August 16, in the Malacca Strait off the coast of Indonesia, authorities seized 14,077 kg of Methamphetamine with a value of USD 658,442 (equivalent to ₹5.40 crore).

Meanwhile, in the Red Sea off the coast of Saudi Arabia, authorities seized a massive 2,250,000 Amphetamine pills with a value of USD 56.2 million (equivalent to ₹461 crore) on August 17.

Other seizures included 320 kg of Amphetamine tablets and 2,980 kg of Hashish with a value of USD 20 million (equivalent to ₹164 crore) in the Gulf of Oman on August 30; 676 kg of Methamphetamine with a value of USD 8,943,772 (equivalent to ₹73 crore) in the Malacca Strait off the coast of Malaysia on September 10; and 870 kg of Methamphetamine with a value of USD 16,624,350 (equivalent to ₹136 crore) in the Arabian Sea on October 9.

Yaba–Syabu seizures

In July and September of 2022, Malaysia and Bangladesh were the locations of several instances of illegal drug trade. On July 4, in the Celebes Sea off the coast of Malaysia, 32 kg of Syabu were seized with a value of USD 397,830 (equivalent to ₹3,26,22,060). Later that month, on July 29, 15.58 kg of Syabu were confiscated in the Malacca Strait, also in Malaysia, with a value of USD 150,190 (equivalent to ₹1,23,15,580). In Bangladesh, on August 16, authorities seized 170,000 Yaba pills in the Bay of Bengal, while on September 22, 90,000 Yaba tablets and 10 packets of Yaba cigarettes with a total value of USD 262,247 (equivalent to ₹2,15,04,254) were intercepted in the same area and on October 9, 80,000 Yaba pills and 2.12 kg of Crystal Meth with a value of USD 1,296,387 (equivalent to ₹10,63,03,734) were seized in the Bay of Bengal.

Captagon seizures

On June 29, 2022, in the Red Sea region of Saudi Arabia, 3.5 million pills of Captagon were seized. A month later, on July 22, 2022, the same region saw the interception of 15 million Captagon tablets. On August 12, 2022, 1.1 million Captagon pills were confiscated in the Red Sea region. On September 22, 2022, in the Persian Gulf region of UAE, authorities seized 170 kg of Cannabis, 46 kg of Crystal Meth, and 50,000 pills of Captagon.

Cannabis seizures

Mauritius, Sri Lanka, India, Oman, Indonesia, and South Africa were some of the countries/regions involved in the drug seizures, during the period from July 1, 2022, to October 8, 2022. In Mauritius/Indian Ocean, 3.5 kg of Heroin and 1.7 kg of processed Cannabis worth USD 1,331,390 were seized on July 1. On July 9, in Sri Lanka/Gulf of Mannar, 4.280 kg of Cannabis worth USD 15,717 were confiscated. Additionally, on July 10, 109 kg of Cannabis worth USD 400,267 were seized in the same region. On July 11, 22.14 kg and 203 kg of Cannabis, valued at USD 18,171 and USD 166,612, respectively, were confiscated in Sri Lanka/Gulf of Mannar.

In Sri Lanka/Palk Bay, 50.90 kg and 30 kg of Cannabis worth USD 186,399 and USD 112,582, respectively, were confiscated on July 15 and July 18. On July 16, in Malaysia/Malacca Strait, 300 kg of Cannabis worth USD 213,675 were seized. In Sri Lanka/Palk Bay, a significant amount of 575.6 kg of Cannabis worth USD 2,151,357 was confiscated on July 19. On the same day, Oman/Gulf of Aden seized 158 kg of Hashish, 2,300 tablets of psychotropic drugs, Cannabis, and Opium worth USD 213,675.

On July 27, in India (Palk Strait), two separate incidents involving 60 kg of Cannabis each were reported. On August 2, 47.24 kg and 363 packets of Cannabis, valued at USD 176,296 and USD 669,231, respectively, were seized in Sri Lanka (Gulf of Mannar) and India (Arabian Sea). On August 3, 49.38 kg of Cannabis worth USD 176,296 were confiscated in Sri Lanka (Gulf of Mannar), followed by 34.038 kg of Cannabis worth USD 125,762 in Sri Lanka (Palk Bay) on August 4.

On August 18, 73 kg of Cannabis was seized in the Gulf of Oman. On the same day, 363 packets of Cannabis worth USD 669,231 were confiscated in the Arabian Sea. On August 19, 93.20 kg of Cannabis worth USD 74,766 were seized in Sri Lanka (Indian Ocean), while on August 27, 18 packs of Cannabis were reported in Indonesia (South Pacific Ocean). On August 29, 3.2 kg of Cannabis was seized in the same region.

On September 5, 37 kg of Cannabis worth USD 30,448 were confiscated in Sri Lanka (Palk Bay). On September 7, in Mauritius (Indian Ocean), 12.6 kg of Cannabis (Zamal) worth USD 188,239 were seized. On September 13, in Sri Lanka (Gulf of Mannar), 434 kg of Cannabis worth USD 355,034 were confiscated. On September 23, two packets of Cannabis were seized in Indonesia (Philippine Sea). On October 3, 58 kg of Cannabis worth USD 197,835 were seized in Mauritius (Indian Ocean), followed by 217 kg of Cannabis worth USD 136,892 in Sri Lanka (Palk Bay) on October 5.

On October 6-7, five packets of Cannabis were reported in Indonesia (Philippine Sea), and on October 8, 479 packets of Cannabis (dagga) were seized in South Africa (Indian Ocean).

Hashish seizures

On September 3, a shipment of Opium, psychotropic tablets, and Hashish weighing 470 kg was seized in the Gulf of Oman.

On September 28, Omani authorities made another significant seizure, this time intercepting a whopping 7,200 kg of Hashish with an estimated value of 10 million US dollars.

The sheer scale of this operation is staggering and highlights the persistent and pervasive nature of the illicit drug trade in the region.

On the 6th and 10th of October, Kuwait and the Gulf of Oman were once again the sites of significant seizures with 131 kg of Hashish discovered in Kuwait, while 5,000 kg of Hashish along with 800 kg of Methamphetamine were seized in the Gulf of Oman.

Combating Drug Menace

THE ROAD AHEAD—ERADICATING DRUG ABUSE

The bitter truth is that drug addiction is an escalating issue in India, accompanied by a substantial surge in drug trafficking. While drug seizures across different states in India may offer some encouragement to drug enforcement agencies, it also underscores the extensive prevalence and exploitation of drugs and highlights the widespread abuse of drugs pan-India.

It's imperative to note that eradicating drug abuse and drug menace is a long-term process that requires sustained effort and commitment by the government as well as the community. It requires a multi-faceted approach that involves individuals, families, communities, and policymakers.

Eradicating drug abuse and plummeting the drug menace in our country requires a multifaceted approach that includes prevention, treatment, law enforcement, community engagement, and an intra-state, inter-state, multi-agency as well as international cooperation.

Prevention efforts should focus on education and awareness campaigns, especially for young adults. Accessible, affordable and effective treatment, drug deaddiction centres should be provided for individuals struggling with drug abuse.

Law enforcement with stern hands should enforce drug laws and regulations to deter drug trafficking and distribution. Laws should be suitably amended for drug addicts and the judiciary should ensure that drug addict or user is sent to rehabs and not jail as they are sick and not criminals.

"Sick or a Criminal?"

Sent to rehabs; not to jails

For the last four decades, the NDPS Act has been in force, and over this period, the majority of people facing criminal charges and imprisonment are those who have been caught using drugs. In the past five years, more than 2.5 lakh people were booked under NDPS Act, and a significant proportion of them were drug addicts or drug users.

> Hence, as a nation, we need to reassess this matter from a more humane, understanding and compassionate perspective. We have to shift our attitude towards drug addicts and come up with a method which distinguishes between those who are traffickers and users.

In other words, we ought to investigate the option of decriminalizing drugs for those struggling with addiction. In short, we should explore the idea of decriminalizing drugs when it comes to drug addicts.

Our current legislation does provide for the possibility of an addict being freed on bail/bond for rehabilitation and detoxification treatment, however, there are several loopholes in the law that require reform. This law is inadequate and requires amending. Around the world, many countries have decriminalized drugs in some form or another. It is essential to make the distinction between drug legalization and decriminalization.

Let's have a look at the current legislation for addicts.

"Addict" as per the NDPS Act

The following sections outline the authority of the central government to regulate and make rules regarding various aspects of the NDPS Act, including the form of bond to be executed by a convicted addict released for medical treatment. The bond serves as a promise by the individual to appear before the court within one year with a report on the outcome of their treatment and to abstain from committing any offences under Chapter IV of the NDPS Act. This provision emphasizes the government's commitment to ensuring the effective implementation and enforcement of the NDPS Act and its provisions.

According to the definition provided in the NDPS Act of India, an "addict" is a person who has developed a dependence on any narcotic drug or psychotropic substance. The term is used in the context of the NDPS Act to describe individuals who have developed a physical and/or psychological reliance on drugs or substances that have mind-altering effects. Under the provisions of the NDPS Act, Section 4 mandates that the central government shall take necessary measures to prevent and combat the abuse of and illicit trafficking of narcotic drugs. This section specifically highlights, among other measures, the importance of identification, treatment, education, after-care, rehabilitation, and social reintegration of individuals struggling with addiction.

The World Health Organization (WHO) substituted the terms "addiction" and "habituation" with **"drug dependence,"** although these old terms are still prevalent.

Addiction refers to the repetitive use of psychoactive substances that lead to recurring or chronic intoxication, an urge to consume the substance, difficulty in voluntarily ceasing or reducing substance use, and an unyielding resolve to obtain the drug through any means necessary. Drug dependence includes various physiological, behavioural, and cognitive symptoms, showing a need for repeated drug consumption and impaired control over substance use, even with negative outcomes. In contrast, psychological or psychic dependence indicates a lack of control over drug use.

As per the provisions of the NDPS Act of India, Section 39 provides for the power of the court to release certain offenders on probation. When an individual is found guilty of an offence related to a small quantity of a narcotic drug or psychotropic substance and is determined to be an addict, the court may choose to direct the individual, with their consent, to undergo medical treatment for de-toxification or de-addiction at a government recognized hospital or institution. The individual must enter into a bond in the form prescribed by the central government, promising to appear before the court within one year with a report on the outcome of their treatment, and abstaining from committing any offence under Chapter IV of the NDPS Act. This provision is based on the court's consideration of the offender's age, character, background, and physical or mental condition.

As per the provisions of the NDPS Act of India, Section 64A provides immunity from prosecution to addicts who voluntarily seek treatment for de-addiction. An individual who is charged with an offence under Section 27 or with offences involving a small number of narcotic drugs or psychotropic substances and who voluntarily seeks medical treatment for de-addiction at a government-recognized hospital or institution shall not be subject to prosecution under Section 27 or any other section related to offences involving small quantities of these substances. However, this immunity from prosecution can be withdrawn if the individual does not complete the treatment for de-addiction.

As per the provisions of the NDPS Act of India, Section 76(2)(c) grants the central government the power to make rules regarding the form of bond to be executed by an addict convicted of an offence related to a small quantity of a narcotic drug or psychotropic substance, who has been released for medical treatment under Section 39(1) of the NDPS Act. The rules may prescribe the bond to be executed by the convicted addict before their release after receiving due admonition under Section 39(2) of the NDPS Act.

A flaw in the law

The existing legislation on drug abuse has a few limitations when it comes to rehabilitating drug addicts. One limitation is that the legislation only allows for rehabilitating individuals who are considered "addicts". This means that if an individual who has used drugs for the first time is apprehended, they may not be eligible for rehabilitation under the law.

Additionally, the law requires that individuals who are addicts must voluntarily seek rehabilitation. If they do not, judges cannot force them to go to rehab. This creates a problem because some addicts may not be in the right state of mind to voluntarily seek treatment and may need someone else to intervene and help them get the treatment they need.

Moreover, agencies often invoke various sections of the law that make it impossible for drug users to seek the benefit of rehabilitation.

This can discourage drug users from seeking help and may cause them to continue using drugs, which can have a detrimental effect on their health and well-being.

To address these limitations, there is a need to amend the law to recognize drug addicts or users as sick people who need treatment, rather than as criminals who need punishment.

This would help to ensure that drug addicts or users can access the help they need to overcome their addiction and lead healthy life.

The legislation only allows sending addicts who voluntarily seek rehabilitation to receive treatment. If an individual who has consumed drugs for the first time is apprehended, they may not be eligible for rehabilitation. Additionally, if an addict refuses to seek voluntary rehabilitation, the judge cannot force them to receive treatment. This is a flaw in the law.

Further, there has been a practice by the agencies of invoking various sections of the NDPS Act, on such addicts or drug consumers, which makes it almost impossible for those drug consumers, to seek the benefit of rehabs.

This lacuna in the law needs to be immediately removed. The law needs to be suitably amended. The courts should have the power to send such drug users to rehab for treatment.

> An addict or a drug consumer should be seen as a sick person who needs treatment and not punishment. **Let's ensure they are sent to rehab and not to the jails.**

The touch-starved rehabs: Lack of infrastructure, lack of human touch

In India, Heroin is the most commonly used opioid, followed by pharmaceutical opioids and Opium. The current prevalence of opioid use is 2.06 per cent, and approximately 0.55 per cent of the population requires assistance for opioid use issues. Cannabis products are used by around 2.8 per cent of the population, with bhang being more popular than Ganja or Charas. An estimated 0.66 per cent of the population needs help with Cannabis use problems. The NDDTC of the AIIMS submitted a report on the "Magnitude of Substance Use in India" in 2019, which confirms the above findings.

India is a vast nation with a population of almost 1.4 billion, with an estimated 6.8 crore people into drug abuse, more than 1.6 crore people are struggling with drug-related problems, they are addicts and in need of help.

> In plain words, these 1.6 crore individuals are sick and need immediate dedicated deaddiction treatment.

Despite consistent governmental attention and effort, every high-level discussion on this subject has resulted in new policies and guidelines.

While the intention of these policies is admirable, the implementation is hindered by insufficient infrastructure, as the country lacks adequate rehabilitation and detoxification centres to support such a large section of a society grappling with drug and substance abuse.

There are few rehabs run by states, under the national scheme known as Integrated Rehabilitation Centres for Addicts (IRCAs), however, the overall capacity is far less than the actual requirement looking at the magnitude of drug abuse and day-to-day growing drug menace.

The dearth of rehabilitation centres has given rise to opportunistic individuals looking to profit from the situation. Sadly, the result is that drug addicts who lack the financial means are left to suffer without treatment, while a selection of lavish, five-star resort-style rehabs exist that charge exorbitant amounts of up to five lakh per month.

What is even more disheartening is the fact that several de-addiction centres fail to comply with the norms set by the government under the National Action Plan for Drug Demand Reduction (NAPDDR).

These centres lack the necessary infrastructure, adequate medical professionals, and staff to manage their patients effectively and safely.

On the other hand, there are some so-called deaddiction centres, that ill-treat the drug addicts and lack the human touch to heal them.

Drug abuse problems can get worse if there aren't enough good centres to help people get off drugs and get better.

> When people who are addicted to drugs don't have access to good treatment and support, they may be more likely to keep using drugs and deal with the bad effects.

It's important for governments and healthcare providers to recognize the need for high-quality de-addiction and rehabilitation centres and invest in developing and expanding these services. This cannot be done by just giving funds to addiction treatment programs but by making sure there are more trained professionals in this field and making sure that people who need treatment can get it seamlessly and at a low cost.

In addition to making sure that there are adequate treatment options, it's also important to work on preventing drug abuse to lower the number of people who use drugs. This can include education programmes that inform people the truth about the risks and effects of drug use, as well as interventions that deal with things like mental health problems or socioeconomic stressors that can lead to drug use.

Addressing the issue of drug abuse requires a multifaceted approach that includes both efforts to prevent drug abuse and to help people who are already using drugs. By making it more accessible for individuals to get good treatment and addressing the reasons why people use drugs, we can help people get over their addictions and reduce the damage that drug use does to our communities. Let's remember, the human touch that heals.

FULL BODY TRUCK SCANNERS (FBTS)

The recent smuggling of a massive consignment of narcotics through the Indo-Pak border in Punjab has sparked concern about the efficiency of the customs department, the reliability of multi-agency intelligence, and the security of India's first Integrated Check Post (ICP). Despite the presence of two full-body truck scanners at the ICP, the truck loaded with 600 kg of narcotics and rock salt granules managed to pass through undetected. The incident has raised suspicions about the involvement of influential individuals in the smuggling of 584 kg of Heroin into India. The value of the drugs is estimated to be around ₹2,600 crore in the international market. The customs officials discovered the smuggled drugs, after unloading the rock salt granules bags

> The FBTS is a vital tool in enhancing border security and preventing the smuggling of illegal goods such as fissile material, narcotics, and contraband.

The FBTS can scan approximately 30 to 180 trucks per hour while the mobile X-ray container scanners can scan approximately 20 trucks per hour. It takes around 20 seconds to scan a truck using FBTS and approximately three minutes to scan a truck using a mobile X-ray container scanner.

The announcement of the installation of five full-body truck scanners at various international borders in India was made in 2017. These borders included ICP Attari, Uri-Islamabad, Poonch-Chakandabagh (Indo-Pakistan borders), Raxaul (Indo-Nepal), and Petrapole (India-Bangladesh).

In September 2021, the FBTS at ICP Attari became operational. Unfortunately, the FBTS installed at ICP Attari is no longer functioning and has been scrapped by the responsible agency. This situation raises concerns about the security and efficiency of the customs department and the need for new and effective measures to prevent smuggling and other illicit activities.

Recently, as per reports, eight mobile X-ray container scanners were added to the existing four X-ray container scanners previously installed by the customs department at various major ports to improve the scanning process and reduce the time required for scanning containers. Most of the ports are equipped with specialized equipment to handle different types of goods.

Installation of Full Body Truck Scanners (FBTS) and Radio Detection Equipment (RDE) for non-intrusive scanning, the implementation of Automatic Number Plate Recognition (ANPR) and real-time data collection capabilities are the need of the hour.

> The implementation of these technologies can help in the early detection and prevention of drug trafficking, organized crime, and terrorism.

Container Scanning Facility

India is bordered by water on three sides, with the Bay of Bengal located on the east coast, the Arabian Sea on the west, and the Indian Ocean to the south. Its coastline spans over 7,000 kilometres, with the state of Gujarat accounting for nearly 1,600 kilometres.

> The country is home to 13 major ports and 205 minor and intermediate ports. Some of these major ports process container cargo that exceeds five million TEU per year, which equates to nearly 100,000 containers being handled each week.

Given the large volume of containers, it is impossible for human inspectors to thoroughly examine each one for contraband or drugs. This is where technology can play a vital role, and therefore it is imperative that state-of-the-art container scanners are installed at every port. The latest state-of-the-art container scanning facility at JNPT has improved efficiency, allowing for quicker inspections and clearance of cargo containers. This highlights the importance of using advanced trace detection systems to prevent the entry of illegal substances and contrabands into the country.

> Drug trafficking on marine routes has increased exponentially. A similar container scanning facility needs to be installed at all major and minor ports.

Full-body Scanners to screen arrivals

With the large number of people entering the country daily, it is difficult to stop cases of smuggling based only on profiling and tips from insiders. The Customs department should also be provided with a dedicated full-body scanner to screen arrivals at all international airports.

> The implementation of body scanners would significantly aid in the detection of foreign objects (drugs and gold) inside a human body, effectively reducing the smuggling of illegal goods through human carriers and drug mules.

The Future is Technology and AI: Drug Testing Kits

Advanced technology: Modern Mobile drug detection system

The current methods for drug detection are outdated and in need of replacement with a modern mobile drug detection system. This new system should incorporate automated colourimetric detection for both drugs and be equipped with testing swabs that can detect even trace amounts. State agencies responsible for anti-narcotics, as well as customs, DRI, and NCB, must be equipped with these mobile digital kits, which can detect a variety of drugs including narcotics, stimulants, depressants, hallucinogens, and other substances of abuse.

The new technology offers the advantage of automated detection, eliminating the need for human interpretation and minimizing the possibility of human error. The results screen displays all relevant information, including the analyzed pouch, date and time, and GPS location, with the option to add notes and pictures. PDF reports can be generated and shared for evidence collection.

> **The latest drug testing kits** have the facility and capability which include the process of detecting and analyzing drugs present in seized materials or biological samples such as body fluids (blood, saliva, urine), hair, or other tissues.

The purpose of this analysis is to determine the presence of one or more psychoactive substances.

> The departments should also be equipped with a drug testing system that utilizes saliva samples for fast and accurate results.

The process of collecting saliva is now simple, hygienic, and painless, taking less than a minute. The results are displayed clearly on the instrument screen, reducing the likelihood of Human error or misinterpretation.

AI-based Data Analytics

In the era of AI and chatbots, the traditional record keeping, and outdated reporting systems require a complete overhaul. A modern and efficient system is needed to keep up with the latest technology and advancements in data management and analysis. The new system should be able to streamline the process of storing, organizing, and retrieving information, and provide valuable insights to help decision-making.

The need for an AI-based Big Data Analytics System (BDAS) to tackle the drug problem is pressing. With the growing amount of digital information, the aim is to extract valuable insights from this data to combat crime, address new and emerging threats, and disrupt the flow of drugs and Narco money.

This solution can gather data from a multitude of sources, including internal data, CDR (call data records), and IPDR (internet protocol detail record), and will easily integrate money trail data. This information can be used to create statistical and analytical models that provide valuable insights for investigative and operational purposes and enable intelligence-led decision-making.

The project's objective is to establish a digital repository or knowledge bank, integrate ingestion modules for internal databases, and utilize machine learning modules to analyze unstructured information. The solution should also have multi-dimensional link analysis tools, the ability to understand social dynamics within a network, and the capability to analyze historical investigation reports. It must be user-friendly with a simple interface while retaining advanced analytical capabilities.

> The goal must be to have a solution for analyzing historical investigation reports, case diaries, intelligence reports, and other documents for better organization, search, and linking of information.

The solution must be secure for sharing and reporting information and should be able to address the majority of analytical needs throughout the investigation process.

The aim is to have a solution with a user-friendly interface that can be easily used by domain experts, with minimal IT support. The solution should be easy to use but still, maintain its advanced analytical capabilities. It should support combating drugs, with a platform incorporating the latest technology and advanced analytical tools to provide intelligence and insights and create a safe and drug-free society for the people of India.

Justice Delayed is Justice Denied

The trend noticed in cases filed under the NDPS Act is that more cases are registered for the personal use of narcotics than for trafficking. The intention of the NDPS Act is to have efficient laws to handle illegal drug use and trafficking, as well as user rehabilitation.

> However, the high number of outstanding cases contradicts the goal of enacting the law. Prolonged hearings that last years would be unfair to the accused in such instances. The large number of pending cases, which reached 2.72 lakh in 2020, remains a cause for concern.

According to the NCRB Crime in India (CII–2020) study, the number of complaints filed under the NDPS act has increased in recent years, with a substantial increase of more than 25 per cent in 2017 and 2018 compared to prior years. In 2019, the number of instances filed under the NDPS legislation increased even further, with over 72,000 cases being documented. However, long hearings and many ongoing cases weaken the legislation's efficacy by preventing prompt justice and possibly leading to abuses for charged people. To accomplish the objectives of the NDPS Act, it is critical to simplify judicial processes and guarantee quick hearings.

> The Supreme Court recently in March 2023, pronounced a pathbreaking and landmark judgement in the case of Mohd Muslim @ Hussain vs. State (NCT of Delhi) in Special Leave Petition (Criminal) No. 915 of 2023, which emphasized the importance of concluding **trials speedily**, especially in cases where special laws have stringent provisions.

The court pointed out that a plain and literal interpretation of the rigorous conditions under Section 37 of the NDPS Act would make granting bail impossible. However, the grant of bail on the ground of undue delay in trial is not fettered by Section 37, and the court emphasized the importance of Section 436A of the Code of Criminal Procedure, which requires the accused to be enlarged on bail if the trial is not concluded within specified periods. The court held that special conditions as enacted under Section 37 can only be considered within constitutional parameters when the court is reasonably satisfied that the material on the accused is not guilty.

There are two important issues which need to be addressed by our judicial system.

> The judicial system needs to address two critical issues. Firstly, it's concerning drug users and addicts. The cases booked for the possession of drugs for consumption must be decided within 72 hours of arrest, and drug users or addicts must be sent to rehabilitation centres, with or without their consent, as per the earlier discussions on this subject.

This amendment to the NDPS Act is necessary to ensure that drug users receive timely and appropriate care and support.

It is crucial to note that sending drug users to jail or granting police or judicial custody to them is not a viable solution to the problem of drug abuse. Instead, rehabilitation and treatment should be the primary focus of the justice system to address drug addiction and promote recovery.

> A complete overhaul of the judicial system is required in this regard to ensure that drug users receive the appropriate care and support they need to overcome their addiction.

As per the reports, the majority of the cases booked, and persons arrested under the NDPS Act are those who are found with drugs for their personal consumption. The criminalization of drug use often leads to stigmatization and discrimination against drug users and addicts, which can prevent them from seeking help or accessing essential services. Therefore, it is essential to approach drug addiction as a health issue rather than a criminal offence and provide appropriate treatment and support to drug users.

The amendment to the NDPS Act proposed here aims to ensure that drug users receive the necessary care and support for their recovery while also addressing the issue of drug abuse. It is a step towards the development of a more compassionate and effective judicial system that prioritizes the well-being and rehabilitation of drug users and addicts.

In conclusion, the Indian judicial system must take a more holistic and humane approach to address drug addiction and drug-related crimes.

> By focusing on rehabilitation and treatment rather than punishment, we can ensure that drug users receive the support they need to overcome their addiction and lead healthy, productive lives.

The proposed amendment to the NDPS Act is a step towards achieving this goal and building a more equitable and just society for all.

> The second and most important judicial reform is time bound disposal of the NDPS cases. Unfortunately, the so-called Fast-Track Courts are not so fast.

It's the overall system which is responsible for the same and reforms are needed in all concerned quarters. With the current pace, it will take decades to clear the enormous amount of pending NDPS cases. The government should try and set up a system for time-bound disposal.

Man, Machine, and the Dogs

Drones have become a major factor in the smuggling of narcotics and weapons, creating a challenge that is beyond human capability to tackle. The western frontier of Punjab and Jammu and Kashmir is already in the grip of a narco war, with nameless and faceless drones dropping packets of Heroin.

The number of drones seen in Punjab coming from Pakistan to bring drugs, guns, explosives, and ammunition has quadrupled.

> In the year 2021, 67 drones were discovered. Since January 2022, about 254 drones have been seen, 22 of which have been shot down by the BSF.

As per reports, 311 drones were sighted over the whole western border, including Gujarat, Rajasthan, Punjab, and Jammu & Kashmir.

> The need of the hour is to have drone jammers installed at all sensitive border locations.

We need to have a specialist 'hit' squad at the border that downs a drone using rifle fire or jamming technology. As per reports, there have been a few instances where electronic devices placed by the army in border regions have blocked Pakistani drones. The device was shot down after it became motionless in the air. More such advanced technology devices are required to be installed.

Moreover, it's a fact that we are facing several "maritime challenges" due to its long coastline and that Heroin seizures have surged many in the past few years. To address this issue, the Indian Coast Guard should consider using drones for coastal surveillance and interception.

K-9 the elite canine squads

A Nigerian woman passed through all checkpoints at Mumbai International Airport, including Customs officials and screening devices, but Pinky discovered something suspicious in her shoes. Crores worth of drugs were confiscated. Pinky, the sniffer detector canine and proud member of the K9 team nabbed the drug trafficker where man and machine failed. Her friends stationed at different key air and land checkpoints were not far behind.

> Celin, a cute Retriever, sniffed and detected 15 kg of Hashish at Kolkata Airport, while Drager sniffed and uncovered 532 kg of Heroin at the ICP in Attari.

Although the BSF is deploying various measures to tackle the threat of drones dropping packets of narcotics and weapons, the drones are still flying at a higher altitude, dropping packets, and returning. The BSF has trained sniffer dogs and is relocating street dogs to detect drones Experts have stated that the drones dispatched from Pakistan in recent times are challenging to detect at night since they do not make any buzzing sounds and have an unblinking appearance.

> To aid in detecting the drones, the BSF has trained sniffer dogs like Frooti, who can identify the faint sound of a drone and run towards it, and they are also relocating street dogs to the border for drone detection.

Dogs have a hearing capacity beyond humans. They can hear the faintest sound that a human ear cannot gauge.

In high-altitude regions of Jammu and Kashmir's Gulmarg, dogs are not just strays for the locals and the army, but they also serve as companions and early warning systems for soldiers patrolling the LoC. These canines lead the way for soldiers, warn them of any potential dangers ahead, and are cared for as if they were part of the soldiers' families, irrespective of the weather conditions.

> K9-Customs and Nar-K9 are a squad of trained detector canines who specialize in identifying a broad variety of narcotic substances such as Hashish, Heroin, Methaqualone, Amphetamines, Cocaine, Ephedrine, Hashish oil, and Ganja.

A dog's olfactory nerves provide it with exceptional detecting abilities.

The process involved includes right from the selection of pups to the grooming and training. Once the pup is selected, a microchip is inserted in his body to monitor the same. A special schedule for eight months of training along with a full-time dedicated dog handler is done.

Today we need more such K9 squads to monitor public places like railways and public transport as well as important entry and exit points in the states.

Where the man and machines fail, K9 are the most reliable.

Dream of a Drug-Free Nation: Some Positive Steps

Nasha-Mukt Bharat

The government has acknowledged the mounting and rampant growth of the drug menace in the country and has taken significant positive measures to address the issue. The restructuring of Narcotics Coordination (NCORD) is a pivotal move to improve coordination between central and state agencies, thereby enhancing the effectiveness of law enforcement agencies in curbing drug trafficking.

The development of the NCORD portal, an all-in-one platform for drug-related information, is a crucial step towards creating a centralized database that can be easily accessed by law enforcement agencies.

This portal can provide real-time updates on drug-related incidents and facilitate the analysis of drug-related data, leading to the development of more effective strategies to combat drug trafficking.

The NCB and ICJS have collaborated to establish the National Integrated Database on Arrested Narco Offenders (NIDAAN) database to monitor and track the activities of detained narco offenders. Through this database, insights into the patterns and trends of drug trafficking can be obtained, resulting in more effective and targeted law enforcement strategies. The ICJS was established by the Supreme Court e-committee to allow for the smooth transfer of data and information between various sectors of the criminal justice system, including courts, police, jails, and forensic science laboratories, through a unified platform.

> In addition, the establishment of the Nar-K9 pool as a national asset at the NCB is a significant advancement in the detection and seizure of illegal drugs.

The utilization of trained sniffer dogs can vastly improve the ability of law enforcement agencies to detect drugs, and the Nar-K9 pool can enable the sharing of resources and expertise for drug detection throughout the country.

> The launch of MANAS, a dedicated 24x7 national narcotics helpline, is a crucial measure towards providing aid to drug users and their loved ones.

The helpline can offer information on drug abuse prevention and treatment, as well as link drug users to support services like counselling and treatment centres.

The initiatives taken by the central government in combatting drug trafficking and abuse are commendable. These measures can enhance the capabilities of law enforcement agencies, improve access to information and resources, and provide assistance to drug users and their families.

> The war on drugs has just begun and it's a long way to go. The fight against drug abuse is a never-ending battle, and we have a long road ahead of us. We need a strong hand with a soft heart.

What is required is a firm yet compassionate approach, one that employs a resolute hand in dealing with drug traffickers through the implementation of the rule of law, while simultaneously maintaining a humanitarian outlook towards those who are addicted and suffering from this drug menace.

THE ENDLESS DEBATE: DECRIMINALIZATION, DEPENALIZATION, AND LEGALIZATION

Voices on various forums have been raised from time to time to decriminalize drugs in India. On the concepts of depenalization, decriminalization, and legalization, there is no consensus as to what they mean, however, it is beneficial to gain an understanding of the different ideas which they signify.

Broadly speaking, decriminalization refers to the removal of criminal penalties for a particular behaviour, but it may still result in fines or civil penalties. Depenalization refers to the removal or reduction of criminal penalties for certain behaviours or actions. Legalization, on the other hand, refers to the complete removal of all legal penalties for a particular behaviour, making it fully legal and regulated. The specific meanings of these terms can vary depending on the context and the specific behaviour or substance in question.

A school of thought maintains that under the international drug control conventions, small drug-related offences, such as selling drugs to maintain personal drug use or to survive in a marginalized environment, can be considered drug-related offences of a "minor nature". In such cases, individuals should receive rehabilitation opportunities, social support, and care instead of punishment. This approach recognizes the underlying reasons behind drug-related offences and seeks to address the root causes of drug use and drug-related criminal behaviour through a public health approach rather than a punitive one. This aspect of the law needs to be explored by the lawmakers of our nation.

> Many countries have either depenelized or decriminalized or legalized the use of certain types of narcotic drugs, especially Marijuana (Cannabis), either for medical purposes and/or recreational purposes. In the USA, the majority of the states have moved forward in this direction. Canada has been at the forefront. Thailand is the latest to enter this regime.

The recent proclamation announced by the US President, granted pardon to US citizens and permanent residents convicted of simple Marijuana possession, stating no one should be jailed for it. The US President requested the health secretary to review the scheduling of Marijuana under federal law, as it is currently classified under Schedule I of the Controlled Substances Act, which is meant for the most dangerous substances, higher than fentanyl and Methamphetamine.

The implementation of drug laws and policies varies among different countries and even within states or regions of the same country. Despite being signatories to UN conventions and treaties on drug laws, many countries have adopted their own approach to drug use, possession, and trade. For instance, in the United States, federal law and state laws may have different approaches to drug policies.

In Thailand, although the law permits the use of Cannabis for medical purposes, the reality on the ground is that there is widespread use of the substance for recreational purposes.

A similar situation exists in Amsterdam, where there is a culture of using "coffee cafes" for recreational Marijuana drug use, despite the substance being technically illegal. The varying approaches to drug policies highlight the complexity of the issue and the need for ongoing discussion and examination of the effectiveness of different approaches.

The signatory countries are obligated under international law to take measures to reduce the supply of and demand for controlled drugs while also ensuring adequate availability for medical and scientific purposes and respecting human rights.

There is no mandate whatsoever to promote the use and abuse of drugs for recreational purposes. Unfortunately, many nations are setting a wrong precedent, which gives rise to this unnecessary and never-ending debate.

Epilogue-Bibliography-Works Cited References

Epilogue

As I reflect on the writing of this book *India Drugged*, I feel a strong sense of urgency and responsibility. The book was not just an exercise in academic research or literary pursuit, but it was a call to action. The drug problem in India is not just a statistic or a news headline; it is a harsh reality that affects millions of people throughout the country. That's the reason I subtitled it ***An Eye Opener.***

Through this book, I have attempted to provide a comprehensive overview of the drug scenario in India, covering various states and regions, and offering insights into the types of drugs and their effects on the human body and mind. I have also delved into the shadowy world of drug smuggling, the chemistry and economics of drugs, and the global drug scenario.

My aim was not just to provide information but to create awareness, spark a conversation and initiate dialogue.

Writing this book was a challenging task that demanded extensive research, and analysis and it was a task that was worth undertaking. I felt a sense of responsibility to use my knowledge and experience to shed light on the drug problem in India and to offer recommendations for creating a drug-free nation.

As a former NCB officer, I have always been committed to fighting against drug abuse in India. I have seen the devastating effects of drug abuse on individuals, families, and communities. But I have also seen the positive impact of action and the power of prevention and treatment.

Through *India Drugged*, I hope to inspire policymakers, law enforcement agencies, and the general public to act and create a drug-free India. The book provides recommendations for eradicating drug abuse, providing treatment to addicts, and strengthening law enforcement agencies. It also highlights the role played by technology in combating drug trafficking and the need for a multi-pronged approach.

In conclusion, I would like to say that *India Drugged* is not just a book; it is a call to action. It is a reminder that the drug problem in India is real, and it requires urgent attention. I hope that this book will serve as a guide for creating a drug-free India and that it will inspire individuals, communities, and governments to act.

Together, we can create a better future for ourselves and for generations to come.

– **Monish Bhalla**

GLOSSARY OF DRUG LEXICON AND ABBREVIATIONS

1. **Amphetamine-type stimulants**: It is a group of substances composed of synthetic stimulants controlled under the Convention on Psychotropic Substances of 1971 and from the group of substances called Amphetamines, which includes Amphetamine, Methamphetamine, Methcathinone and the Ecstasy-group substances (3,4-Methylenedioxymethamphetamine (MDMA) and its analogues).

2. **Amphetamines**: It is a group of Amphetamine-type stimulants that includes Amphetamine and Methamphetamine.

3. **Annual prevalence**: The total number of people of a given age range who have used a given drug at least once in the past year, divided by the number of people of the given age range, and expressed as a percentage.

4. **Coca paste (or coca base)**: An extract of the leaves of the coca bush. Purification of coca paste yields Cocaine (base and hydrochloride).

5. **Crack Cocaine**: A Cocaine base obtained from Cocaine hydrochloride through conversion processes to make it suitable for smoking.

6. **Cocaine salt**: Cocaine hydrochloride

7. **Drug use**: Use of controlled psychoactive substances for non-medical and non-scientific purposes, unless otherwise specified.

8. **Fentanyls**: Fentanyl and its analogues

9. **New psychoactive substances**: Substances of abuse, either in a pure form or a preparation, that are not controlled under the Single Convention on Narcotic Drugs of 1961 or the 1971 convention, but that may pose a public health threat. In this context, the term "new" does not necessarily refer to new inventions but to substances that have recently become available.

10. **Opiates**: A subset of opioids comprising the various products derived from the Opium poppy plant, including Opium, Morphine, and Heroin.

11. **Opioids**: A generic term that refers both to opiates and their synthetic analogues (mainly prescription or pharmaceutical opioids) and compounds synthesized in the body.

12. **Problem drug users**: People who engage in the high-risk consumption of drugs. For example, people who inject drugs, people who use drugs on a daily basis and/or people diagnosed with drug use disorders (harmful use or drug dependence), based on clinical criteria as contained in the *Diagnostic and Statistical Manual of Mental Disorders* (fifth edition) of the American Psychiatric Association, or the *International Classification of Diseases and Related Health Problems* (tenth revision) of WHO.

13. **People who suffer from drug use disorders/people with drug use disorders**: A subset of people who use

drugs. Harmful use of substances and dependence are features of drug use disorders. People with drug use disorders need treatment, health and social care and rehabilitation.

14. **Harmful use of substances:** Defined in the *International Statistical Classification of Diseases and Related Health Problems* (tenth revision) as a pattern of use that causes damage to physical or mental health.

15. **Dependence:** Defined in the *International Statistical Classification of Diseases and Related Health Problems* (tenth revision) as a cluster of physiological, behavioural and cognitive phenomena that develop after repeated substance use and that typically include a strong desire to take the drug, difficulties in controlling its use, persisting in its use despite harmful consequences, a higher priority given to drug use than to other activities and obligations, increased tolerance, and sometimes a physical withdrawal state.

16. **Substance or drug use disorders:** Referred to in the *Diagnostic and Statistical Manual of Mental Disorders* (fifth edition) as patterns of symptoms resulting from the repeated use of a substance despite experiencing problems or impairment in daily life as a result of using substances. Depending on the number of symptoms identified, substance use disorder may be mild, moderate or severe.

17. **Prevention of drug use and treatment of drug use disorders:** The aim of "prevention of drug use" is to prevent or delay the initiation of drug use, as well as the transition to drug use disorders. Once a person develops

a drug use disorder, treatment, care and rehabilitation are needed.

18. **EMCDDA**: European Monitoring Centre for Drugs and Drug Addiction

19. **INCB**: International Narcotics Control Board

20. **UNODC**: United Nations Office on Drugs and Crime

21. **NCB**: Narcotics Control Bureau

22. **NIA**: National Investigation Agency

23. **CBN**: Central Bureau of Narcotics

24. **BSF**: Border Security Force

25. **ATS**: Anti-Terrorism Squad

26. **DEA**: Drug Enforcement Agency

27. **IDMA**: Indian Drug Manufacturer Association

28. **NPS**: New psychoactive substances

29. **ATS**: Amphetamine-type substances

30. **CBCS**: Codeine-based cough syrup

31. **LSD**: Lysergic acid diethylamide

32. **THC**: Tetrahydrocannabinol

33. **Tor**: The onion router

34. **MoSJE**: Ministry of Social Justice and Empowerment

35. **CMF**: Combined Maritime Forces

36. **IFRC-IOR**: Information Fusion Centre-Indian Ocean Region

37. **MHA**: Ministry of Home Affairs

38. **ILO**: International Liaison Officers

39. **WHO**: World Health Organization

40. **NDDTC**: The National Drug Dependence Treatment Centre

41. **AIIMS**: All India Institute of Medical Sciences

42. **IRCAs**: Integrated Rehabilitation Centres for Addicts

43. **NCRBL**: National Crime Record Bureau

44. **INCB**: International Narcotics Control Board

45. **IB**: Intelligence Bureau

46. **FPO**: Foreign Post Office

47. **PRI**: Panchayat Raj Institutions

48. **NAPDDR**: National Action Plan for Drug Demand Reduction

49. **LoC**: Line of Control

50. **ICP**: Integrated Check Post

51. **NCORD**: Narcotics Coordination

52. **NIDAAN**: National Integrated Database on Arrested Narco Offenders

BIBLIOGRAPHY

Works Cited—References

1. *Open Government Data (OGD) Platform India.* (n.d.). Open Government Data (OGD) Platform India; data.gov.in. https://data.gov.in/resource/drug-head-wise-seizures-under-ndps-act-during-2019

2. *Open Government Data (OGD) Platform India.* (n.d.). Open Government Data (OGD) Platform India; data.gov.in. Retrieved May 31, 2022, from https://data.gov.in/resource/seizures-under-ndps-act-during-2020

3. *Open Government Data (OGD) Platform India.* (n.d.). Open Government Data (OGD) Platform India; data.gov.in. Retrieved May 31, 2022, from https://data.gov.in/resource/state-wise-arrested-persons-under-ndps-act-year-2016-upto-octoberfromministry-home-affairs

4. *Crime in India 2020 | National Crime Records Bureau.* (n.d.). Crime in India 2020 | National Crime Records Bureau; ncrb.gov.in. Retrieved May 31, 2022, from https://ncrb.gov.in/en/Crime-in-India-2020

5. Ashok, A. (2019, June 25). *Golden Triangle.* Golden Triangle; indianarmy.nic.in. https://indianarmy.nic.in/writereaddata/CLAWS/Goldenper cent20Triangle.html

6. *Crime In India | National Crime Records Bureau.* (n.d.). Crime In India | National Crime Records Bureau; ncrb.

gov.in. Retrieved May 31, 2022, from https://ncrb.gov.in/en/crime-india

7. *WDR 2021_Booklet 1.* (n.d.). United Nations : Office on Drugs and Crime; www.unodc.org. Retrieved May 31, 2022, from https://www.unodc.org/unodc/en/data-and-analysis/wdr-2021_booklet-1.html

8. *Crime in India 2020 | National Crime Records Bureau.* (n.d.). Crime in India 2020 | National Crime Records Bureau; ncrb.gov.in. Retrieved May 31, 2022, from https://ncrb.gov.in/en/Crime-in-India-2020

9. *Home.* (n.d.). Narcotics Control Bureau; ncb.cyberchallenge.in. https://ncb.cyberchallenge.in/

10. *UN commission reclassifies Cannabis, yet still considered harmful | | UN News.* (2020, December 2). UN News; news.un.org. https://news.un.org/en/story/2020/12/1079132

11. *UN commission reclassifies Cannabis, yet still considered harmful | | UN News.* (2020, December 2). UN News; news.un.org. https://news.un.org/en/story/2020/12/1079132

12. *World Drug Report 2021.* (n.d.). United Nations: Office on Drugs and Crime; www.unodc.org. https://www.unodc.org/unodc/en/data-and-analysis/wdr2021.html

13. *World Drug Report 2019.* (n.d.). United Nations: World Drug Report 2019; wdr.unodc.org. https://wdr.unodc.org/wdr2019/

14. *World Drug Report 2020.* (n.d.). United Nations: World Drug Report 2020; wdr.unodc.org. https://wdr.unodc.org/wdr2020/index2020.html

15. *Drug rehabilitation—Wikipedia. (2020, November 1). Drug Rehabilitation—Wikipedia.* https://en.m.wikipedia.org/wiki/Drug_rehabilitation#

16. Dhawan, A., Rao, R., Ambekar, A., Pusp, A., & Ray, R. (n.d.). *Treatment of substance use disorders through the government health facilities: Developments in the "Drug De-addiction Programme" of Ministry of Health and Family Welfare, Government of India.* PubMed Central (PMC). https://www.ncbi.nlm.nih.gov/pmc/articles/PMC5659092/

I express my gratitude to all the sources that have helped me in my research and writing. I appreciate the authors of the books, articles, and other sources for sharing their expertise with the world.

I have examined and studied numerous such references and sources during the course of writing my book. To view the complete list of Bibliography, Works Cited, and References sources, readers can access the QR code or link provided.

Link – https://taxolegal.com/index.php/books-2/